Golf

GETAWAYS

from CLEVELAND

Golf
GETAWAYS from CLEVELAND

John H. Tidyman

GRAY & COMPANY, PUBLISHERS
CLEVELAND

Maps by Ken Gross, Rustbelt Cartography

Gray & Company, Publishers
1588 E. 40th St.
Cleveland, OH 44103-2302
www.grayco.com

ISBN 1-886228-39-6
Printed in the United States of America
First printing

Yoshiro Takaoka, M.D., Ph.D., is my All-American. A dozen years ago he studied X-rays of my brain. He wasn't the first. The first few neurosurgeons who looked said the situation was inoperable and likely fatal. Dr. Tak saw something the others didn't see.

He saved my life.

Since then, I've been able to study this most remarkable man. He is fiercely proud, yet humble, technically proficient and accomplished, yet steeped in tradition. He stands easily, one foot in Japan, one foot in America. He is Buddhist and Shinto. He loves and cares for his wife and children as well as his colleagues.

And Dr. Tak loves golf.

CONTENTS

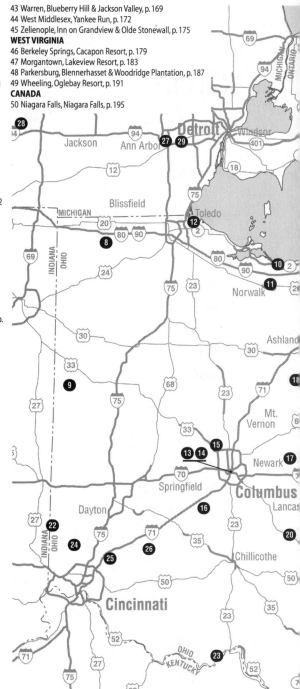

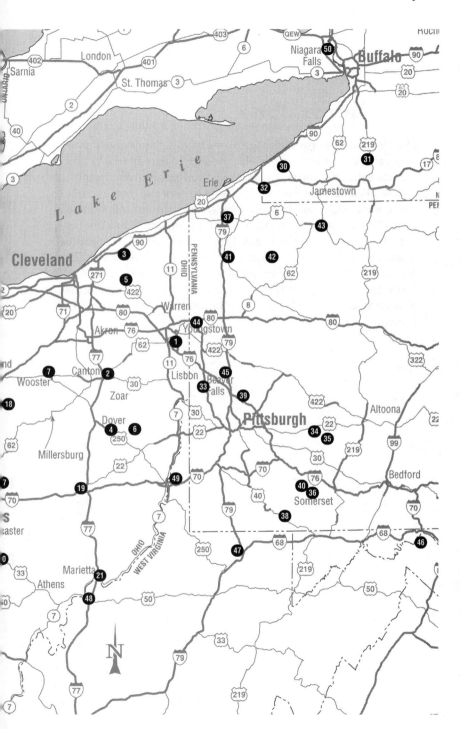

ACKNOWLEDGMENTS

Lisa Metro was the project manager for the two delightful seasons it took to research and write this guide. She found the courses and the lodging, contacted the right people, and made all the necessary arrangements.

Several capable volunteers helped with the research. Some traveled alone, some took spouses, some took golfing partners. All acquitted themselves well and are now members of the Order of the Dimple—perhaps the most exclusive club in golf. They include: Bobby Gainer and his father, Robert Sr.; Terry Meehan; Jonathan Wayne; Karen Fuller; Tim Monroe, PGA; Tracy Monroe; Tim Riordan; David Gray, Steve Wood; Laura Hammel; Rob Mier; Kathy Koch; Terry Uhl; Nancy Peacock; Michele Scheufler; Paul Murphy; Tom Lassar, M.D.; Don Franceski; Bill Close; and Tom Livingston.

INTRODUCTION

There are all kinds of golfers, and, I have now discovered, there are all kinds of golf getaways to serve them.

Some getaways are perfect for four guys who have been playing and traveling together for years—guys who want 36 holes a day, big steaks for dinner, and poker chips to play with before bedtime.

Other getaways are wonderful for families, offering diversions like nature studies, hiking trails, even sleeping in a log cabin to complement the golf—or to entertain for those along for the trip who don't play the game.

There are getaways perfect for golfers who also like shopping, romance, or antique hunting. (Golf applies itself with chameleon-like ease.)

This book collects 50 of them—and it's a pretty diverse lot.

The best news, for those of us who can't jet off to Myrtle Beach for the weekend: there are a *lot* of really good golf getaways just a couple of hours away by car from anywhere in Northeast Ohio. Close enough and easy enough to plan that you could take these short weekend trips without much (or in some cases any) advance planning.

The getaways are organized in two major sections. The first includes getaways in the state of Ohio; the second includes getaways in other states and in Canada.

The Ohio section is divided into five geographic areas: Northeast, Northwest, Central, Southeast, and Southwest. Within each geographic area, getaways are listed alphabetically by the town they are in.

Each getaway is described in three parts.

An at-a-glance section gives basic facts—location, driving time, price range—so you can decide quickly if you want to read more. (Cost is rated on a scale of $ to $$$. The cost can vary a lot, depending on how much you like to pamper yourself, but this rating should give a fair idea of how these trips compare with one another on average.)

Then there's a lengthier description of the accommodations, a restaurant that we tried, and of course the golf course(s).

Finally, we list the practical details (phone numbers, addresses, pricing, directions, etc.) you'll want when you're ready to plan your trip.

Many of the hotels and inns are also fantastic places for corporate outings, so I've also included information about the kind of business and meeting facilities they offer.

At the end of each getaway, you'll find a map to give you an idea of where in the state the town is located.

Information may have changed since this book was printed, so be sure to call ahead to double check details before you set out.

While 50 getaways sounds like a lot of golf (and it is), there are still more nearby golf getaways we didn't get to or don't yet know about. If you have one you'd like to see published in future editions, please send the information to the publisher.

OHIO

BOARDMAN, OH
MILL CREEK &
RESERVE RUN

Close by, lots of golf choices, and a hotel that caters to corporate golf outings

LOCATION: Northeast OH
DRIVE TIME: 1–2 hours
COST: $$$
....
STAY: Holiday Inn, Boardman, OH
PLAY: Mill Creek Golf Course, Boardman, OH
Reserve Run Golf Course, Youngstown, OH
NEARBY: Youngstown State University

If you're thinking of taking a golf getaway and Youngstown is not on your mind, maybe it should be. We took a short golf trip to Youngstown, stayed at the Holiday Inn Youngstown South (actually in Boardman), and played a couple of courses.

We'd go again in a minute.

The drive is just an hour and a half. While a Holiday Inn isn't exotic, this hotel is first rate. The golf packages are excellent values. The restaurant, T.J.'s, gets good grades for food, service, decor, and value. The rooms are well-appointed and very comfortable.

And the golf here is served up like a Sunday buffet: you can choose from 11 courses that pair up with the hotel for packages.

It was just a couple years ago that general manager Brent Reynolds asked Dan Walsh to come from the Holiday Inn in Hermitage, Pennsylvania, where he was fast building a golf package trade, and work his same magic in Boardman.

Dan Walsh is to golf packages what shiners are to perch fishing. His first year he booked maybe 100 golf packages. The second year? Seventeen hundred. The guy knows golf packaging.

"We're a major hotel for corporations," Walsh said. "We take our programs to corporations to let them see how well we handle meetings of all sorts and tie in great golf." The first floor is meeting rooms and a huge banquet room.

It's a major hotel for individuals, too.

As soon as we had the bags unpacked we went to T.J.'s for a pre-golf lunch. I had a steak salad that reminded me of the great steak salad at the old Theatrical Grill in downtown Cleveland. Except this was even better. How good was it? I'll tell you what: Unless I'm in T.J.'s, I may never order another steak salad. If only a Cleveland restaurant could find a steak with that much flavor and a chef who knew how to grill it perfectly rare! It was set on top of French fries, which sat on top of the salad.

Walsh brags about the kitchen staff. John Fabian, the executive banquet chef, has been there a decade. Don Young, the executive chef, has been there almost a decade and a half. T.J.'s is an independent restaurant in the hotel.

Players and companies come from Cleveland, Buffalo, and all points in between. They get the big things—T.J.'s restaurant and Handel's ice cream across the street—and the little things—logo balls, bags of tees, and sun visors.

Handel's? It's an ice cream stand across the street from the hotel. According to *USA Today*, it's one of the best in the country. It was started in 1945 when Alice Handel scooped up ice cream she made and sold it at her husband's gas station, at the corner of Market Street and Midlothian in Youngstown. The first few batches included fruits from Alice's backyard garden. The quality hasn't declined much since then. They make the stuff fresh every day, now including yogurts, of course, with the freshest ingredients available. And when you ask for a couple scoops, they deliver scoops as if they knew you and liked you.

But we came to play golf, not promote Boardman. (Though Boardman *is* a very clean and bright town. Wait till you see.)

THE GOLF

The two courses we played are right down the street and only minutes from the Holiday Inn.

To play Mill Creek is to play legendary golf design; it offers a pair of wonderful Donald Ross courses that look easy and play tough. Ross insisted on accuracy, especially with the irons, and that demand is evident here. The course features small greens (sometimes deceptive but more often straightforward), judicious use of sand bunkers, and gorgeous hardwoods lining virtually every hole. The north course plays 6,173 yards and the south 6,302. They are joined by a great big friendly clubhouse. Even if you don't have time to play, this is a nice place to hang out and listen to golfers lie.

While we were there, we also made it to Reserve Run Golf Course. Only 6,162 yards from the back tees, Reserve is short by design. The terrain rolls over 150 acres, and it's a challenging course that provides a big serving of fun.

Reserve got its start when owners Bob Saleman, Scott MacDonald, and Rick Vernal decided to convert a one-time strip mining site. Designer Barry Serafin was pleased to find two deep quarries he could use as a water source. The course is fully irrigated.

(Some veteran miners here say that pieces of heavy equipment rest on the bottom of the quarries—victims of flooding caused when underground springs were hit.)

Serafin's little gem opened in the summer of 1999 and has been very well received by players. Two reasons for the applause might be Nos. 7 and 8.

NO. 7 IS A PAR 4 OF ONLY 375 YARDS, BUT WHAT YARDS!

No. 7 is a par 4 only 375 yards, but what yards! This dogleg right has a steep hill dominating the entire right side and a lake runs down the left.

No. 8 is a 219-yard par 3, and every one of those yards is over water. That, we hasten to add, is from the back tees; the day we played, the tee had been moved up to 185 yards. There is a strip of terra firma on the right side for those who would rather bail than swim.

Throughout the course there are four sets of tees, so no hole should be so intimidating as to make a player anxious.

The home hole is a long one, especially for this short course. It moseys along 430 yards to an elevated green.

Par is 70 and position golf is the game.

We stayed late after grabbing a couple drinks and relaxing on the deck that overlooks Nos. 6 and 7.

GOLF HERE IS SERVED UP LIKE A SUNDAY BUFFET: 11 COURSES PAIR UP WITH THE HOTEL FOR GREAT PACKAGES.

ACCOMMODATIONS

Holiday Inn   (330) 726-1611
7410 South Ave., Boardman, OH

ROOMS: 153; **SUITES:** 7

ROOM RATES: $155+   **PAYMENT:** checks, MC, VS, AX, DIS, DC

SPECIAL RATES: discounted rates upon availability

RESTAURANTS: T.J.'s Lounge (avg. entree $16.95)

RESORT AMENITIES: indoor pool, health club, hot tub, cable TV/movies, room service, smoking rooms, non-smoking rooms, conference facilities

CONFERENCE/BUSINESS MEETING FACILITIES: 10,000 square feet of meeting space including a ballroom accommodating 300

GOLF

GOLF PACKAGE RATES: $120–$220 for 1–2 days and 1–3 rounds

PACKAGE INCLUDES: food/beverages, cart rental; weekend packages available; Sun–Thu packages available

COURSES:

Mill Creek Golf Course   (330) 758-2729
West Golf Dr., Boardman, OH

Reserve Run Golf Course   (330) 758-1017
625 E. Western Reserve Rd., Youngstown, OH

OTHER ATTRACTIONS NEARBY

Youngstown State University, Youngstown Playhouse, Youngstown Symphony, Butler Art Institute, Mill Creek Park, Yellow Duck Park, outlet and retail shops

DIRECTIONS

I-80 west to exit 232 for SR-7; north on SR-7; right on US-224; right on South Ave.

CANTON, OH
TAM O'SHANTER
& THE LEGENDS

*Must-play courses that should be on
every serious Cleveland golfer's list*

LOCATION: Northeast OH
DRIVE TIME: 1–2 hours
COST: $$

. . . .

STAY: Holiday Inn, Canton, OH
PLAY: Tam O'Shanter,
NW Canton, OH
The Legends of Massillon,
Massillon, OH
NEARBY: Pro-Football Hall of Fame

Why is it that so many Northeast Ohio golfers have yet to play The Legends of Massillon and the Hills and Dales courses at Tam O'Shanter? If you can find I-77, you can find these courses. Is it a case of, "yeah, yeah, I'll get around to it" but never do? A shame, because there is very good golf to be had, and it is very close by.

Maybe it's because it's so close that we think of it as a day trip—and a long drive for an afternoon of golf. In that case, a stay at the Belden Village Holiday Inn may be the ticket. As part of an overnight, these courses are much more doable.

In all our travels for this book, no place was more crowded, more commercial, more given to neon than Belden Village, where we stayed at the Holiday Inn. The view from our room was of the parking lot—not as romantic as we might have wished, but . . . well, we're here for golf, right?

Our room was big and comfortable with the usual accouterments: cable television, mini-fridge (empty), sofa-bed, roomy bathroom with coffee maker. Putting the coffee maker in the bathroom sounds like one of those decisions made by a committee. We had failed to pack toothpaste, and when we asked at the desk, they produced a smile and a complimentary tube. We know this is S.O.P., but we so rarely forget anything except the kids, and service of this sort is kinda fun.

The hotel restaurant is a no-frills, family friendly joint. No surprises on the menu—standard American fare. But the staff was surprisingly friendly and pleasant.

THE GOLF

Tam O'Shanter is lovely, with two scenic courses, a magnificent club-house, and a noteworthy history. The Dales opened first, in 1928, and three years later, the Hills course opened. As if to slap the Depression in the face, developer T. K. Harris brought in two pro players from the Western Open, Walter Hagen and Gene Sarazen, to play the dedication round. Despite Prohibition, there was liquor all around.

The Hills course was designed by Merle Paul, the Dales by Leonard Maycomber, construction superintendent for Donald Ross when the de-signer from Dornoch, Scotland, created Canton Brookside in the early twenties.

On the Dales, Nos. 4 and 5 are representative. No. 4 is a straight, 411-yard par 4. Trees line both sides of the fairway the last couple hundred yards. On the No. 5 tee, it's a blind shot. This fairway does more than rise: there is a steep hill in the middle. Clearing the hill is not as difficult as it appears, but missing can be costly. On the back side, No. 15 is one of those holes that the designer found: a 405-yard par 4, it tumbles into a valley, rights itself and climbs the side of a hill. The tee shot is blind, so making sure the players in front have cleared the landing area is impor-tant. To them, at least.

The Hills is a shorter, more open course. No. 5 is that most confound-ing of golf holes: a good, short par 5. It is only 434 yards, but the fairway narrows on this dogleg right and O.B. stakes line the entire right side. In the final 150 yards, the rough on both sides rise, and the hole resembles a riverbed. Tall trees close in near the green, and hardwoods form a

handsome backdrop for approaches. The home hole is a short and easy par 4 of only 267 yards. If you haven't won the match by this time, don't plan on winning it here.

Next up was Legends of Massillon. Now, how could we not love Legends? Massillon spent $6 million on this golf course! And what a course. Canadian John Robinson is responsible for the layout here, honored with four and a half stars from *Golf Digest.*

Since it opened in 1995, it has done more than get good reviews: it has grown by an additional nine holes. The three nines: North, South, and East were created by dividing the original layout into six-hole segments and then adding three new holes to each.

It can play as long as 7,000 yards and as short as 4,600 yards. Good driving range here, and a great short game practice area.

The fairways, tees, and greens are bent grass; the lush rough is a bluegrass and rye mix. Landing areas are generous, and conditioning is just what you would expect from a course where Craig Immel is the head honcho. Immel was the original pro at Quail Hollow, the award-winning pro at Westwood Country Club, and one of the founders of StoneWater Golf Club. He is a native of Massillon.

NOW, HOW COULD WE NOT LOVE LEGENDS? MASSILLON SPENT SIX MILLION ON THIS GOLF COURSE

This course is so nice that next time we're going to start on the North course at daybreak and play until the sun goes down or we pass out. Every stick in the bag gets a workout here, and it's the thinking golfer who scoops up the skins. Not only are there 83 bunkers divvied up, but on 22 of the 27 holes, there is water. Lots of water.

The North course has the great finishing hole, a long par 5 that has to avoid sand right and left off the tee. It doglegs around a huge pond, so .. . feelin' lucky?

On the South course, it was another par 5 that grabbed us and held on: 525 yards and water crosses at 260 yards. Once over the creek, the hole turns right before arriving at a lake and a peninsula green.

It's the second hole on the East course, a 400-yard par 4 that has to avoid bunkers on both sides and then carry a pond in front of the green. The water is almost at the green, so a forward tee position is for suckers only.

Approaching this green gives you the prettiest scene on the course: a huge grove of pine trees stands behind the green.

These are three tracks every northeastern Ohio golfer should play a few times.

ACCOMMODATIONS

Holiday Inn   (330) 494-2770
4520 Everhard Rd., Canton, OH

ROOMS: 193; **SUITES:** 1

ROOM RATES: $85–$229   **PAYMENT:** checks, MC, VS, AX, DIS, DC

RESTAURANTS: Belden Village Bar and Grill

RESORT AMENITIES: outdoor pool, health club, cable TV/movies, room service, pets welcome, smoking rooms, non-smoking rooms, conference facilities

CONFERENCE/BUSINESS MEETING FACILITIES: ballroom with more than 3,200 square feet of space, accommodating up to 400 guests. An additional meeting room accommodates up to 75. Two hospitality suites are also available.

GOLF

GOLF PACKAGE RATES: $128–$274/person for 7 days and 1–3 rounds

PACKAGE INCLUDES: food/beverages, cart rental; weekend packages available; Sun–Thu packages available

COURSES:

Tam O'Shanter   (800) 462-9964
5055 Hills and Dales Rd., NW Canton, OH

Legends of Massillon   (330) 830-4653
2700 Agusta Dr., Massillon, OH

OTHER ATTRACTIONS NEARBY

Pro-Football Hall of Fame, Harry London Chocolate Factory, McKinley Museum and Memorial, Belden Village Mall, Amish country

DIRECTIONS

I-77 south to exit 109 for Everhard Rd.; right to first light; on left.

CONCORD, OH
RENAISSANCE
QUAIL HOLLOW
RESORT

*Upscale and relaxing with a choice of
tracks by big-name designers*

LOCATION: Northeast OH
DRIVE TIME: Under 1 hour
COST: $$$

....

STAY: Renaissance Quail Hollow
Resort, Concord, OH
PLAY: Quail Hollow Golf Course,
Concord, OH

Renaissance Quail Hollow Resort's two wonderful golf courses, the Weiskopf-Morrish course (on everyone's list of top 100 courses) and the VonHagge-Devlin course (where the Hogan-Nike-Buy.com Open is held) are well known but little played by the natives.

The resort just finished a $17 million renovation and remodeling. The detail is apparent at first glance: the lobby is decorated in marble, stone, and wood. It evokes a contemporary, natural feel—perfect for upscale visitors. It appears much of the business is ... well, business of the corporate variety. There is a full-service business center with computer hookups, facsimiles, and business concierge. A lounge just off the lobby had comfortable Morris chairs and large tables, and it appeared some business conferees had taken the meeting into the lounge for a more casual atmosphere.

The rooms here don't disappoint. Each is spacious, well appointed, and has cable television, in-room movies, and even Sega gaming equipment. All the usual amenities were there, including a fresh copy of *USA Today* at the door in the morning.

The fitness center here has more than some neighborhood YMCAs have: several state-of-the-art treadmills, Stairmasters, recumbent bicycles, weight machines, and limited free weights. The swimming pool is substantially longer than the usual, so doing our forty laps in the morning was a good workout. Just above the pool is the whirlpool, which could easily fit ten adults without it seeming unnatural. There is also an outdoor swimming pool and full-service day spa.

What used to be the Quail Room is now CK's Steakhouse, the initials coming from Charley Klaskin, a major investor as well as devout fan of fine wines. The wine list has 130 selections. The chef de cuisine is Jason

Brust, and some of his offerings were more than good—they were memorable. The entire menu was created by him, so kudos to the chef for the incredible Maryland crab cakes, the porcini-dusted Chilean sea bass, the rack of lamb, and the double-cut pork loin chop. On the side he offers a lot, but the dish that remains in the mind's eye is mashed potatoes. The flavors blend perfectly, neither overwhelming the other. Not just any mashed potatoes but lobster-mashed potatoes. If we would have known about his mashed potatoes before ordering, we would have asked the sommelier, "What do you suggest for two plates filled with lobster-mashed potatoes?" My Reason for Living suggested the sommelier might suggest, "The door, sir." But I don't think so.

It wasn't necessary, but we ambushed the dessert tray and came up with a five-layer carrot cake, noteworthy for its texture and flavor, and a hot fudge pecan ball, noteworthy because a hot fudge pecan ball *should* be noteworthy! Here's how much we enjoyed dinner: we're going back just to have dinner.

In addition to the resort, there is fishing, winery tours, and quaint restaurants and pubs nearby. The concierge knows all … and tells all.

THE GOLF

Love the pro shop. No bargains here, but if we were to pick up a few pieces of clothing or equipment to memorialize our stay, the selection here is first rate.

The Devlin-VonHagge course, built in 1975, has an edge to it. It threads its way through mature hardwoods, and we played in spectacular early October foliage—a melange of brilliant reds, oranges, yellows, and greens. Landing areas are generous, and the rough extracts a penalty. The real appeal here is the sloping and slick greens. These greens roll 10.5–11.0 on the Stimpmeter—faster than most resort courses and much faster than average players are used to playing. Once we got used to them, they were a delight.

The signature hole here is No. 9, a long dogleg left and downhill. The drive has to get out there 230 yards for the player to see the green, which is significantly downhill and well trapped. We found disaster on one of golf's shortest holes, the 110-yard No. 12. It looks like a pushover, but when the cup is in the front of the green, and the greens are this fast … well, let's skip the bloody details.

The Weiskopf-Morrish course is the pride and joy of Quail Hollow. We say that, because it was better conditioned and maintained. The differences between the two courses are not easily discerned by average players. They are about the same length, and the slopes and course ratings are very similar. The VonHagge design is more straightforward, the

Weiskopf a little slicker. At Weiskopf's course, the bunkering is more menacing, the hazards more exaggerated.

One of Weiskopf's design signatures is the short par 4, and No. 7 is a very good one: 261 yards, and it can be reached easily. Going for the green had only one risk, and that was a deep trap on the left side of the green. But we'd rather be there than bouncing along beyond the green anyhow. Our favorite hole was No. 12, a downhill, dogleg par 4 where the trees down the left side guide the drive. The second shot has to contend with sand and water, and that's to get to a two-tiered green. No. 14 has to be a heartbreaker. This par 5 stretches to 585 from the blues, and the third shot has to carry marsh. A par here calls for a beer, and not one of your domestics, but an import!

Almost forgot. We played with a member, and were glad for his company and counsel. Playing a course for the first time means being at the mercy of the designer, and little guidance is provided here. But this nice man had a lot of local knowledge he was happy to share with us.

One more wonderful surprise was the bartender, who we met as soon as we had cleaned our shoes and were relaxing in the bar; he was just as enthusiastic about golf as we. It cemented a fine day of golf.

THESE GREENS ROLL FASTER THAN AVERAGE PLAYERS ARE USED TO PLAYING.

ACCOMMODATIONS

Renaissance Quail Hollow Resort   (800) 468-3571
11080 Concord-Hambden Rd., Concord, OH

ROOMS: 176; **SUITES:** 6

ROOM RATES: $119–$350   **PAYMENT:** checks, MC, VS, AX, DIS, DC

RESTAURANTS: C.K.'s Steakhouse (avg. entree $21)

RESORT AMENITIES: indoor pool, outdoor pool, health club, sauna, hot tub, cable TV/movies, room service, smoking rooms, non-smoking rooms, babysitting service, conference facilities

CONFERENCE/BUSINESS MEETING FACILITIES: more than 15,000 square feet of space; 15 function rooms; conference center; 5,000-square-foot ballroom

GOLF

GOLF PACKAGE RATES: $199/single; $279 double for 1 day and 1 round

PACKAGE INCLUDES: food/beverages, cart rental

COURSE:

Quail Hollow Golf Course   (800) 468-3571
11080 Concord-Hambden Rd., Concord, OH

OTHER ATTRACTIONS NEARBY

Lake Erie fishing charters, Holden Arboretum, Little Thunder Golf Course (18-hole championship golf course designed especially for children), Lake County Wine Country

DIRECTIONS

I-90 east to SR-44 (Auburn Rd.); left on Auburn; continue until Concord-Hambden Rd.; on right.

NEW PHILADELPHIA, OH
OAK SHADOWS

To say Oak Shadows is a good-looking course is like saying Slyman's makes a pretty good corned beef sandwich

LOCATION: Northeast OH
DRIVE TIME: 1–2 hours
COST: $

STAY: Schoenbrunn Inn, New Philadelphia, OH
PLAY: Oak Shadows Golf Course, New Philadelphia, OH
Black Diamond Golf Course, Millersburg, OH

This town is about as undistinguished as any American town is ever going to get. (Well, today it is. In 1772 it was very distinguished as Schoenbrunn, the first settlement in Ohio.) The Schoenbrunn Inn, where we stayed, notes on a promotional brochure that the inn is right next to McDonald's. So what? We're not here to gorge on Happy Meals. What we gorged on was Goshen Dairy ice cream. The local dairy, started in 1920, makes wonderful ice cream and serves it at a number of locations. Finishing a long day of golf with a shower, dinner at the Courthouse Cafe on South Broadway, and then dessert at Goshen's—well, it's the stuff of dreams.

And the Schoenbrunn Inn, next to a burger joint or not, is experienced and professional with golf packages. The modern inn is also next door to the Lewis Conference Center, and Inn manager Kathy Landis does a substantial executive trade. She has 66 rooms, some with Jacuzzi baths. The Inn has no restaurant, but in the morning the Pub is transformed to offer a very substantial continental breakfast (with no additional charge).

History is spoken here: Quaker Stadium was the site of Woody Hayes's first game as a coach; John Glenn soloed for the first time at Hary Clever Field; and *Trumpet in the Land* was the first official outdoor drama for the state. Not likely anyone's blood pressure will rise, but still …

Landis has five courses on her package list: Zoar Village GC, Wilkshire Hills GC, Green Valley GC, River Green GC, and Oak Shadows GC. It was Oak Shadows that we came to play. The course's reputation for

physical beauty, exciting design, and great golf challenge has been inching its way north for a couple of years. At Oak Shadows, blood pressures
do rise and pulses quicken.

Landis told us that the owners of a new course, Black Diamond GC in
Millersburg, will become part of her outing package, but when we were
there the course had only 9 holes open. She made a tee time for us, and
we went. Black Diamond's two nines are open now. Black Diamond, in
the heart of Amish country, is the most exciting golf course to open in
Ohio this century.

THE GOLF

After the Schoenbrunners ran the natives off the property, what is
today Oak Shadows was then farmland. In the late 1970s it was strip-
mined; later it was reclaimed. Opened in the fall of 1995, this 200-acre
course was designed by Canadian John Robinson, who also designed the
Legends of Massillon. (I've always had a problem with that name: how
can anything be legendary when it opens?) There are 65 sand and grass
bunkers strewn over the course as well as substantial areas of wetlands.
The view from the clubhouse is wonderful, with much of the course laid
out like a buffet. It plays 3,196 going out from the blues and 3,215 coming back: 6,411, par 72. The gold tees are longer by 600 yards, and the
whites are shorter by 500 yards. The forward tees total 5,207. Included in
the greens fee is a sandwich and beverage at the turn. Nice touch.

To say Oak Shadows is a good-looking golf course is like saying Slyman's corned beef is a pretty good sandwich: this course is cutting-edge
design, a big and beautiful layout, and likely an indication of the type of
courses that will be built for public players in the future.

The opening hole is a big, twisting par 5 accented with water, and No. 2 is the entryway to the Valley of Golf here. Nos. 2 through 8 are played in and around the valley walls. No. 5 is a good example of the striking design: a par 3 of 171 yards. Instead of stacking the tee boxes one on top of another, Robinson stuck them in the side of the valley wall, lining them up horizontally. From any tee, it's a good hole—well-defined and challenging.

On the back nine, No. 13 deserves mention. From an elevated tee, this 362-yard par 4 tumbles steeply downhill before starting around a big, C-shaped lake to an undulating green.

It's difficult to leave Oak Shadows after playing only one round.

A caution here: call the course first to see what's going on. We played behind a junior tournament—need we say more?

Black Diamond GC is a twenty- or thirty-minute drive from New Philadelphia. Much of the ride is two-lane blacktop of gently rising and falling roads that are lined with family farms. This is Amish country, and special care must be taken to watch out for the horse-and-buggies that are a part of it.

The course and driving range have been four years in the making by architect Barry Serafin, from New Albany, Ohio. The entire course opened for play in August, 2001. From the clubhouse, the view of the course looks computer-enhanced—it is that detailed, clear, and colorful. One of the great colors used is the rich tan of wheat. On a number of holes, fields of the earthy grain wave in the breeze. Using wheat (which regenerates itself) as a design tool makes for a bigger, happier bird population.

ON SEVERAL HOLES, FIELDS OF WHEAT WAVE IN THE BREEZE

Only 6,462 from the blue tees, this course demands a great deal from players. Balls, for one thing. Missing the rough means losing a ball. And for the first trip or two around this magnificent track, the penal nature of some of the holes rears up. The terrain rises and falls, sweeps across valleys and around lakes.

The first hole is the signature on the front side, a 523-yard par 5 that incorporates rockwall splitting the fairway and a waterfall behind the green. Nothing wrong with No. 7, either, one of the rare par 6s in golf. With six tee boxes on this hole, it can play from a brief 540 yards to a long, long 700 yards. On the back side, No. 16, a pretty and short part 4 of 374 yards, has a lake on the left and trees on the right. The green on this hole is tiny; leaving the ball on the right side of the fairway allows branches to block the approach.

The slope for the blues is 130; green is 124; yellow is 122; and forward tees are 118. It is not a course for walking.

As seasons come and go, Black Diamond will grow more beautiful. As one of only two courses in Holmes County, it has to draw from Cleveland, Akron, and Columbus, as well as Dover and New Philadelphia. The bet has been placed.

ACCOMMODATIONS

Schoenbrunn Inn   (800) 929-7799
1186 W. High Ave., New Philadelphia, OH

ROOMS: 50; **SUITES:** 11

ROOM RATES: $80–$126   **PAYMENT:** checks, MC, VS, AX, DIS, DC

SPECIAL RATES: seniors, AAA, AARP, government

RESTAURANTS: Schoenbrunn Inn

RESORT AMENITIES: indoor pool, sauna, hot tub, fitness center, cable TV/movies, room service, pets welcome, smoking rooms, non-smoking rooms, conference facilities

CONFERENCE/BUSINESS MEETING FACILITIES: can accommodate meetings and seminars

GOLF

GOLF PACKAGE RATES: $99–$186 for 1–3 days and 1–3 rounds

PACKAGE INCLUDES: cart rental; weekend packages available; Sun–Thu packages available

COURSES:

Oak Shadows Golf Course   (330) 343-2426
1063 Oak Shadows Dr. NE, New Philadelphia, OH

Black Diamond Golf Course   (330) 674-6100
7500 Township Rd. 103, Millersburg, OH

OTHER ATTRACTIONS NEARBY

Schoenbrunn Village, Zoar Village, Warther's Carving Museum, Reeves Museum, Dennison Depot, Amish country, antique shopping

DIRECTIONS

I-77 south to exit 81 for SR-39 (W. High Ave.); left on W. High; on right next to McDonald's.

NEWBURY, OH
PUNDERSON MANOR RESORT

*Cozy, charming, stately ...
and haunted?*

LOCATION: Northeast OH
DRIVE TIME: Under 1 hour
COST: $$

....

STAY: Punderson Manor Resort, Newbury, OH
PLAY: Punderson Golf Course, Newbury, OH
NEARBY: Six Flags Worlds of Adventure

The only thing missing was English accents on the wait staff. Everything else about our stay in Punderson Manor reminded us of a country hotel in the Yorkshire Dales. No prefab Tudor here; Punderson was built in the 1920s by a wealthy businessman, and old-money elegance echoes through the two-story great hall and cozy dining rooms, up the ornate plaster circular staircase, and into 31 charming guest rooms. This state lodge has all the modern amenities. Guest rooms have cable TV with HBO and a fresh, up-to-date, English decor.

Dinner is a charming experience in the paneled dining rooms with original plaster-sculpted ceilings and brass wall sconces. The menu offers enough seafood to make it a tough choice. The sole we had was blessed with a wonderful cucumber-dill sauce, and the blackened ribeye had a spicy Cajun flavor. Feeling vegetarian? The chef will amaze and delight you.

The Manor is haunted. Said to be, anyway. At the front desk is an eight-page history of the ghost sightings.

Punderson was bought by the state in 1948, and the new guest-room wing blends seamlessly with the old design. There are meeting rooms for group retreats and pools indoors and out. The indoor pool was completed in 1999, and its glass walls overlook the glacier-carved lake and forests that wrap around the lodge.

Punderson's location is a fooler: you only think you are in the middle of nowhere. The nearby town of Burton calls itself Pancake Town USA because of its maple syrup production in the spring. They are no Johnny-come-lately. Since 1951, over a million pancakes have been served, covered with 19,500 gallons of maple syrup, nestled next to 87,000 pounds of sausage.

In the fall, Burton hosts an Apple Butter Festival in its Century Village Museum, which includes a blacksmith shop, village square mall, steam powered mini-train ride, and craft and flea market. The area is loaded with antiques shops. Thirty dealers fill the Country Collections Antique Mall in nearby Middlefield, and Auntie's Antique Mall is close by in Parkman.

In the unlikely event you run out of attractions, Lake Farmpark, an open-air science and culture center in Kirtland, is open year round. It is 235 acres and a hands-on reminder of where our food comes from before the emulsifiers, additives, and MSG are added. It is here that the Vintage Ohio Wine Festival is held and the Quilts show and HorseFest, as well. Early in the summer, there is Fiberfest, and we can't figure out if that's for wool or digestion.

THE GOLF

Jack Kidwell designed this course, which opened for play in 1969. Kidwell also created the wonderful layout at Hueston Woods, the home course for Miami of Ohio in Oxford.

The design is intelligent, and the conditioning is first rate. Situated on high, gently rolling terrain, it offers a mix of wide open holes along with some moderately tight holes.

Punderson is a lot of course: 6,600 yards from the whites is much longer than the average player sees. Much of that, however, comes from the par 5s: No. 3 is 550 yards, No. 6 is the same. No. 15 is 571 yards. The home hole is the last of the par 5s; it plays 487 yards. (The blue tees, by the way, stretch out 6,815 yards.)

The first two holes, par 4s of 371 and 364 yards, are eminently playable. They are good warmup holes. No. 3 plays straight, but the greenskeeper, with a deft touch on the mower, plays optical tricks with a wavy line on the right and a straight line on the left of the fairway. There is water left off the tee, but unless a snap hook is your usual drive, it won't come in to play. Great short game will come into play at the green, however. Four traps guard the green, which has plenty of action. It is a lot of golf hole, and walking off with a par here is more than satisfactory.

Nos. 5 and 6 are good holes, the former a par 4 dogleg right of 349 yards (finally, a hole that fits your slice) and the latter a 550-yard par 5 on which the first two shots are essentially blind. The terrain is rising and crests at the 150-yard marker.

No. 8 makes a lot of "best" lists. A downhill dogleg right par 4 of 411 yards, the approach has to carry substantial water.

On the back side, No. 11, a 390-yard par 4, is magnificent. The landing area is generous, but the approach has to clear a lake with willows anchoring both sides. No. 14, a long par 3 of 196 yards, has to carry water as well as hold the green. No. 15, the last of the long par 5s, calls for three good shots to reach the green. At 571 yards, it features deep woods down the right side and a deep, narrow valley cutting across the fairway 200 yards for the green.

Nos. 17 and 18 are tough holes, and we think no match played here is over until it's over. Seventeen is a 402-yard par 4 that bends slightly right, has water left the last hundred yards, and plenty of sand surrounding the green. The home hole is 487 yards, a short par 5 by Punderson standards that plays straight.

AT THE FRONT DESK IS AN EIGHT-PAGE HISTORY OF GHOST SIGHTINGS.

ACCOMMODATIONS

Punderson Manor Resort   (440) 564-9144
11755 Kinsman Rd., Newbury, OH

ROOMS: 57; **SUITES:** 2

ROOM RATES: $110–$199   **PAYMENT:** checks, MC, VS, AX, DIS, DC

SPECIAL RATES: Golden Buckeye, AARP, children stay free

RESTAURANTS: Punderson Dining Room (avg. entree $19)

RESORT AMENITIES: indoor pool, outdoor pool, cable TV/movies, smoking rooms, non-smoking rooms, conference facilities

CONFERENCE/BUSINESS MEETING FACILITIES: complete banquet facilities for up to 130 guests

SPECIAL PROGRAMS FOR CHILDREN: mid-summer activity program

GOLF

GOLF PACKAGE RATES: $245–$319/person for 2 days and 2 rounds

PACKAGE INCLUDES: food/beverages, cart rental; weekend packages available; Sun–Thu packages available

COURSE:

Punderson Golf Course   (440) 564-9144
11755 Kinsman Rd., Newbury, OH

OTHER ATTRACTIONS NEARBY

Six Flags Worlds of Adventure, Holden Arboretum, Lake Farmpark, Century Village Museum, Pioneer Waterland, outlet shopping

DIRECTIONS

from West: I-480 east; east on SR-422; north on SR-44; west on SR-87 (Kinsman Rd.); on left

from East: I-90 east; south on I-271 to Chagrin Blvd. exit; east on Chagrin; at Lander Circle follow SR-87 east (Kinsman Rd.); cross SR-306; on right.

SHERRODSVILLE, OH
ATWOOD LAKE
RESORT

*Big lake, beautiful view, and an
unusually hilly course*

LOCATION: Northeast OH

DRIVE TIME: 1–2 hours

COST: $$$

STAY: Atwood Lake Resort,
Sherrodsville, OH

PLAY: Atwood Resort Golf Course,
Sherrodsville, OH

NEARBY: Pro Football Hall of Fame

If you have two hours to drive and can find I-77, Atwood Lake awaits. And once the interstate clears the industrial landscape of Akron, the ride is beautiful.

The first of many nice surprises here is the lake itself—it's big! It has two marinas, swimming beaches, and a picnic area. There is a lot of room to set up a tent of one sort or another, and camping at Atwood appears to be one of the favorite ways to visit.

We stayed in the lodge—a big wood-and-stone structure similar to many state park lodges. Substantial, comfortable rooms. Every room here has a lake view. Sitting outside watching the sun settle down is a peaceful way to end the day.

In addition to the golf, the resort emphasizes family activities. There are indoor and outdoor pools, a sauna, and a Jacuzzi. The indoor pool features an unusual design: it has the shallow and deep ends attached perpendicularly and offset, thus giving either end of the pool a somewhat isolated feeling. This will appeal to guests without kids. Towels are provided, and nearby is a fitness room with treadmills and Stairmasters, and a game room with a pool table, air hockey, ping pong, and video games. All well and good on a rainy day, but the draw here is the lake. Boats and jet skis are available for rent.

Nearby is Amish country—always a fascinating visit. We traipsed around there after a summer storm washed out our tee time. Also nearby is Zoar Village, once a religious community and now a living museum.

It's worth an hour or two of your time. At night the Zoar Tavern fills up, but its kitchen has nothing on the resort's.

So, let's get to the carving table. The restaurant at Atwood Lake features big picture-windows that provide a good view of the lake. The golf package includes dinner and breakfast, and between the two, lunch seems like overdoing it. The dinner buffet, our waitress told us, is popular with the locals. We can see why. On the Friday night we were there, the table was filled with crab legs, shrimp, and fish. On Saturday night, it groaned under the weight of handsome slabs of prime rib. Perhaps a good way to describe the food here would be upscale comfort—though when we saw duck on the menu, we had to add that it's fairly adventurous, too.

Maybe it's our imagination, but we always find resort waiters and waitresses to be especially nice. It is often more like your older sister or your aunt serving you at a family get-together. The only thing they fail to do is insist you have a second slice of pie.

THE GOLF

It is an unusual course here—at least for us; mountain goats would find it delightful. Listed at a mere 6,000 yards (and that's from the blue tees), it plays shorter. Maybe because the yardage was measured at ground level and with these steep hills, the ball saves many, many steps. We were suspect of the No. 5 hole, a short par 5 of 465 yards, reached in two by one of our party, using a driver and a 5-iron. The player is known for many things, but length off the tee is not one of them.

There were a lot of couples playing the day we teed it up. The forward tees, we noticed, were very fair and the result of some thought.

The feature we found most unusual was the elevated greens. Typically placed at the very top of a hill, the greens are further elevated, sometimes as much as three feet above the fairway. It's not easy to convey the quirkiness of this, but it reminded us of an upside-down cake pan. Was this an architectural style from years ago? To the unprepared, it is bewildering (and we don't say that just because we seek opportunities to use the word "bewildering"). It means that for uphill approach shots to large greens, a walk up and a survey of the green is necessary before planning a shot. Should the approach fall short, players can find themselves on the short end of an escarpment with a two-foot wall in front. Yo! Beware the chili dip! Players will either love or hate these greens. We found them to be charming. But we found humor in mad cow disease, so we're not the ones to judge.

The course is nicely maintained and conditioned, and the old-growth hardwoods add a traditional flavor. Sand is rare here, as is water.

No. 3 is the signature hole, a 625-yard par 5. The view it provides of Atwood Lake is memorable, and it takes three good shots to get on. But the hole was essentially lifeless until we stood on the green and looked to the lake. An inspiring view.

We found No. 12 to be one of the better holes. It's a par 5 dogleg left that provides a chance even for mortals to get on in two. If, that is, they are sufficiently comfortable with the upside-down-cake-pan green.

The golfing facilities are merely adequate. There is a small pro shop and snack bar. Balls and gloves are available, but there is no major display of shirts or souvenirs. There is a driving range, and it slopes down slightly, allowing right-handed players to hit soft draw after soft draw from the mats. No refreshment carts prowl the paths, though there are several vending machines and port-o-lets on the course.

There is a second course here, a nine-hole, par 3, pitch-and-putt lay-out with lighting. Playing at night is not golf, but it is fun.

Atwood is not a destination for great golf, but it should prove very attractive to families who want to include some golf in their vacations. It is convenient, close by, and has very affordable rates.

ACCOMMODATIONS

Atwood Lake Resort   (330) 735-2211
2650 Lodge Rd. SW, Sherrodsville, OH

ROOMS: 104

ROOM RATES: $104–$133   **PAYMENT:** checks, MC, VS, AX, DIS, DC

RESTAURANTS: Bryce Browning (avg. entree $16)

RESORT AMENITIES: indoor pool, outdoor pool, health club, sauna, hot tub, cable TV/movies, room service, smoking rooms, non-smoking rooms, babysitting service, conference facilities, 18-hole GC, lighted Par-3 GC, 5 lighted tennis courts, hiking & biking trails, lighted par 3 course

CONFERENCE/BUSINESS MEETING FACILITIES: nine conference/meeting rooms accommodating 10–350 people, AV equipment available

GOLF

GOLF PACKAGE RATES: Apr–Dec $218/person, double occupancy; May–Oct $238/person, double occupancy for 2 days and 2 rounds

PACKAGE INCLUDES: breakfast & dinner, cart rental

COURSE:

Atwood Resort Golf Course   (330) 735-2211
2650 Lodge Rd. SW, Sherrodsville, OH

OTHER ATTRACTIONS NEARBY

Pro Football Hall of Fame, McCook House Civil War Museum, Elderberry Train, Warthers Carving, Sugarcreek (Amish country)

DIRECTIONS

I-77 to exit 93 for Bolivar/Zoar; east on SR-212; right on SR-542 (Lodge Rd.); on right.

WOOSTER, OH
HAWK'S NEST

Lovely town, lovely inn, and one of Ohio's best courses

LOCATION: Northeast OH

DRIVE TIME: 1–2 hours

COST: $$

STAY: The Wooster Inn, Wooster, OH

PLAY: Hawk's Nest Golf Club, Creston, OH

NEARBY: Wooster College

etting here is easy. South on I-71 most of the way, followed by a hairpin turn or two, and you're there. The Wooster Inn is on the campus of the College of Wooster. Its small rooms are tastefully decorated, and it's so clean you'll think your mother-in-law has been haranguing the maid. Our room, like the dining room, looked over the driving range.

The town of Wooster is beautiful. Lovely frame homes, lots of hardwoods. The inn is small but elegant and tastefully appointed, with towels and linens better than anything we have at home. The bath has no tub, but a big and comfortable shower.

The dining room is wonderful. The emphasis is clearly on quality, not quantity. It was filled to capacity the Thursday night we were there in August. Fish is prominent on the menu here: walleye, salmon, and trout shared billing with a few very nice pastas and a short stack of great steaks.

Other rooms of note here are the billiard room, the alumni room (which seats 40), and the tartan room (which seats 48). The Inn is used often for wedding rehearsal dinners and family celebrations.

Some of the guests were alumni back for a visit, some were townies, others were guests at the hotel. Many would be picked up by bus and dropped off at the Freedlander Theater on campus for the Ohio Light Opera, a decades-old tradition of celebrating Gilbert & Sullivan among others. (The bus is a convenient touch, but the walking from the Inn on a summer night is delightful.)

If light opera is an acquired taste, many fans have acquired it. An un-

usual and fun touch comes from the tradition established at the Savoy Theater in London, where before each Gilbert & Sullivan performance "God Save the Queen" is sung. The audience here rises to sing, and the veterans, of course, know the words. We assumed the odd guest who remained seated and silent was Irish, but we didn't ask.

The production we saw, *The Gondoliers*, was amazing. With a 30-member orchestra, the professional company delighted the sold-out crowd. Of course, light opera is like, uh, heavy opera: the story is not the attraction—the color, the costumes, the lighting, the music, and the dance are the attractions.

THE GOLF

The course adjacent to the Wooster Inn is a nine-hole course. Additional tee boxes make it a slightly different course when played a second time around for 18. It is a tight and hilly course with receptive greens and a lot of blind shots. Playing this with the 3-, 5-, 7-, and 9-irons and a putter would be a very nice way to go around. In addition to the quirky delights of the golf course at the Inn, just down the road, in Creston, is one of Ohio's best public courses, Hawk's Nest Golf Course. It was built by Betty Hawkins, who ran a high-quality cafeteria for many decades. Hawk's Nest has about 17 signature holes, so plan on a wonderful challenge to your game.

Only the first hole is undistinguished. A short par 4, it's a nice warm-up for the excitement that will follow. It's somewhat hilly here, and the hills, like the water and woods, are used well. While it's not an easy course to score on, it's difficult to play without enjoying yourself. Honored by *Golf Digest* and other golf magazines, this course's driving range is noteworthy, and the snack bar isn't anything to sneeze at. Or on.

ACCOMMODATIONS

The Wooster Inn   (330) 263-2660
801 East Wayne Ave., Wooster, OH

ROOMS: 13; **SUITES:** 2

ROOM RATES: $95–$150   **PAYMENT:** checks, MC, VS, AX, DIS, DC

RESTAURANTS: The Wooster Inn (avg. entree $10.95)

RESORT AMENITIES: pets welcome, non-smoking rooms, conference facilities, outdoor track, tennis courts

CONFERENCE/BUSINESS MEETING FACILITIES: meeting rooms available accommodating up to 50

SPECIAL PROGRAMS FOR CHILDREN: College of Wooster athletic events

GOLF

COURSE:

Hawk's Nest Golf Club   (330) 435-4611
2800 E. Pleasant Hime Rd., Creston, OH

OTHER ATTRACTIONS NEARBY

Ohio Light Opera, College of Wooster, Amish country

DIRECTIONS

I-71 south; south on SR-83; south on SR-585; right on Wayne Ave.; on left.

ARCHBOLD, OH
SAUDER VILLAGE

A living history getaway

LOCATION: Northwest OH
DRIVE TIME: 2–3 hours
COST: $$
....
STAY: Heritage Inn at Sauder Village, Archbold, OH
PLAY: Ironwood Golf Club, Wauseon, OH

Okay, okay, we know this is a golf book, but have you ever been to Sauder Village? Not only is this wonderful recreation of an 1830s small Ohio town remarkable and thought-provoking, it's a delightful way to spend an entire day. We think we smiled more while strolling through the Village than we smiled at any other time while researching the book. Sauder Village is so American, so Ohioan, so human, so fascinating, that we promised to return and spend our time even more leisurely, maybe hanging around the jail this time, or Dr. McGuffin's office for a bit, for sure the grist mill, and we'll hang out at Barbara's weaving shop too. We walked and talked with the residents

WE SMILED MORE WHILE STROLLING THROUGH THE VILLAGE THAN AT ANY OTHER TIME WHILE RESEARCHING THIS BOOK

there—dressed in period clothing—about what appeared to be the slow pace. Not a slow pace, one told us, but a world not yet blessed (or cursed?) with modern technology. Everything took longer. We sat in a log schoolhouse and imagined a stern teacher, wool suit and wing collar, lecturing to barefoot kids; stopped in St. Mark's Lutheran Church and wondered what it was like when fire and brimstone were more current; marveled at the time and talent it took to create baskets in the basket shop—and that was when baskets were necessary, not design frills.

The Village was created by Erie J. Sauder, a local farm boy who founded the Sauder Woodworking Company in 1934. It's a nonprofit living history museum that added a great deal to our golf getaway.

We stayed in the Sauder Heritage Inn, a magnificent and impressive 35-room country inn that opened in 1994. It was hard for the Inn to appear aloof, with huge timbers creating a lattice work in the lobby and hand-forged lamps that light the huge room in the evening.

The rooms are big, comfy, and conveniently outfitted with small refrigerators, a recliner, and coffee pots. Big beds, too—either a pair of queens or a king.

The place also has conference rooms and is a great location for reunions. We wish we had finished high school now just so we could suggest the reunion be held here.

THE GOLF

And the golf course? We teed it up 15 minutes away at Ironwood Golf Club in Wauseon, Ohio. A long course from the tips at 6,965, par 72, it also plays a more humane 6,462 from the whites, 5,609 from the golds/seniors, and a challenging 5,306 (par 74) from the ladies tees. The course celebrated its thirtieth birthday last year, and head golf pro Dick Leazier PGA has been at the helm for the last dozen.

The course is relatively flat, features medium-sized greens, and uses no trickery. There are some great old hardwoods defining some of the holes, and ponds come into play on six holes. The wide fairways are lined with bluegrass (so finish your swing!), and there are only twelve sand bunkers here, so the rounds are played at a quick pace.

On the front side, the hole of note is a 152-yard par 3. It looks easy on the scorecard, but the pond in front of the green makes it appear twice that long. On the back, No. 17, a 394-yard par 4, is memorable. While straight, both sides of the fairway feature water.

The snack bar is notable for its weekend fare, which features Swiss steak, meatloaf, and shredded chicken. (We didn't ask about the shredding process and feel even now it is none of our business.) The snack bar's claim to fame is its hand-dipped milkshakes. The classic comes in only vanilla, chocolate, and strawberry. You can find a better shake, but not on planet Earth.

THE WIDE FAIRWAYS ARE LINED WITH BLUEGRASS (SO FINISH YOUR SWING!).

ACCOMMODATIONS

Heritage Inn at Sauder Village   (800) 590-9755
22611 SR 2, Archbold, OH

ROOMS: 35; **SUITES:** 4

ROOM RATES: $98–$149   **PAYMENT:** checks, MC, VS, AX

SPECIAL RATES: seniors over 65, AAA

RESTAURANTS: Barn Restaurant at Sauder Village; Doughboy Bakery at Sauder Village

RESORT AMENITIES: Cable TV, all rooms non-smoking, conference facilities, fitness room, game room, upscale Continental breakfast, guest laundry

CONFERENCE/BUSINESS MEETING FACILITIES: two conference rooms available

GOLF

COURSE:

Ironwood Golf Club   (419) 335-0587
1015 W. Laggett St., Wauseon, OH

OTHER ATTRACTIONS NEARBY

Historic Sauder Village (living history village (seasonal), Candy Cane Christmas Shoppe, Field of Memories Antique Mall, Toledo Zoo, COSI museum, Toledo Museum of Art

DIRECTIONS

I-80 west to exit 25; south on SR-66; left on SR-2; on right.

CELINA, OH
FOX'S DEN

*A gorgeous little town and
a sneaky tough course*

Ah, Celina! Talk about your Axis powers—a German town with Bella's Italian Grill in the heart of the city.

It was slow getting to this wonderful old town almost on the Indiana border, because we followed directions taken off the Internet, which suggested we go west, young man, on I-90 and then south on I-

LOCATION: Northwest OH
DRIVE TIME: 3–4 hours
COST: $$

STAY: Holiday Inn Express, Celina, OH
PLAY: Fox's Den Golf Course, Celina, OH
NEARBY: Grand Lake State Park

75. Not bad, but the construction tie up on I-75 allowed us to get out and practice swinging for a while. We later asked Holiday Inn Express manager Dani Kohler if there was a better way to get home. Heck yeah, she said. Go north on I-75 but only to SR 30 and take SR 30 east all the way to Mansfield. What a delight! The state route is a very old and well-traveled two-lane blacktop that glides between huge fields of corn and soybean, slows a bit when it slips in and out of small towns, then resumes one of the best road trips we enjoyed for the book. Too bad we weren't able to stay on it longer.

The Holiday Inn Express was perfect for us. Very friendly and professional staff, comfortable and spotless rooms, and an indoor pool with a whirlpool on one end. When we lamented not bringing swim trunks, we were pointed toward the Wal-Mart across the street.

This gorgeous town of 10,000 sits on the shores of Grand Lake St. Mary's, and next visit we'll spend some time there. The lake is big and beautiful and was created in 1837 to serve as a reservoir for the Miami-Erie Canal. Seventeen hundred workmen were paid 35 cents a day and a medicinal shot of booze to protect them from malaria, which, if memory serves, is the same package we received as infantrymen in Vietnam. Ah, another time, another war.

We asked for a restaurant recommendation and were sent to the only Italian place in town, Bella's Italian Grill. The owner/creator is Julie Fleck. After working in other cities for a while, Fleck came to Celina because ... well, because she loved Celina. And Celina had a lot, but it didn't have an Italian restaurant. Figures. German Catholics predominate here. So when she acquired this narrow, high-ceilinged saloon, she found a couple good Italian chefs (is that redundant?) including the talented Carol Milazzo to make cannoli, tiramasu, and carrot cake. The stock for the soup is made right here, and the minestrone had more fresh vegetables that the West Side Market in August.

One of the memorable plates served that night on red-checked tablecloths was portabello ravioli covered with Alfredo sauce on one side and the house red sauce on the other. The wine list, moderately priced, favors California and adds three or four Italians.

We got to know our waitress not because we're the type to flirt with tall blondes in white blouses and red aprons, but because she wasn't really a waitress. Well, she was that night, but only because once a month, Julie Fleck turns over the wait responsibilities to non-profit organizations. All the money volunteers make in tips goes to whatever cause they hold most dear.

Not long after our visit, Fleck started looking to move her restaurant to a bigger space. She found it at 1081 West Bank Road, right on Grand Lake in Celina.

THE GOLF

Fox's Den Golf Course, a newer track designed by Jim Fazio, has sneaky water and it is a sneaky tough course. The wind can rush and stall, blow steady or in bursts, move slowly or quickly. Players who can adjust their game to wind conditions will score better here. An example? On No. 3, a 175-yard par 3 from the gold tees, has water left, but the way to play it that day was to hit the ball over the water and allow the wind to bring it back in. It's a fun course that way.

It's a flat and open course, so Fazio had to use water to add challenge. The finishing holes on both nines are good ones. No. 9 is a 398-yard par 4 with water left and sand right. The fairway rises just a bit. And No. 18, a 528-yard par 5, hugs the water on its right side.

Handsome clubhouse here, good-looking driving range, too. On our next trip, this course will be our first stop, and then we'll look at some other, older courses.

ACCOMMODATIONS

Holiday Inn Express   (419) 586-4919
2020 Holiday Dr., Celina, OH

ROOMS: 52; **SUITES:** 13

ROOM RATES: $69–$140   **PAYMENT:** MC, VS, AX, DIS, DC

RESTAURANTS: CJ Highmarks (avg. entree $9)

RESORT AMENITIES: indoor pool, health club, hot tub, cable TV/movies, smoking rooms, non-smoking rooms, conference facilities

CONFERENCE/BUSINESS MEETING FACILITIES: meeting rooms accommodating up to 25

GOLF

COURSE:

Fox's Den Golf Course   (419) 586-3102
1221 Irmscher Blvd., Celina, OH

OTHER ATTRACTIONS NEARBY

Grand Lake State Park (hiking, fishing, swimming, summer festivals & events), El Dora Raceway

DIRECTIONS

I-71 south; west on SR-30; south on SR-775; west on SR-33; right on Haveman Rd.

HURON, OH
SAWMILL CREEK
RESORT

*A quick and pleasant getaway
to a lakeside resort*

LOCATION: Northwest OH
DRIVE TIME: Under 1 hour
COST: $$$
....
STAY: The Lodge at Sawmill Creek
Resort, Huron, OH
PLAY: Sawmill Creek Golf Course,
Huron, OH
NEARBY: Cedar Point Amusement
Park

reat course, great location. We were mightily impressed with nearby Sawmill Creek Resort, in Huron. It is a quick and pleasant ride to this lakeside resort with the Tom Fazio layout.

That's the good news. The unsettling news is that between the two of us, we put on more than three pounds. Not to extrapolate, but if we spent every weekend there, we could get work as sumo wrestlers.

The resort nestles on 235 acres and offers a fascinating selection of indoor and outdoor activities, programs, and packages.

The main building—and heart of the complex—is the Lodge, recently renovated and today reflecting the art and lifestyle of the original inhabitants, woodland Indians.

The walls are covered with Indian rugs, snowshoes, and artifacts including arrowheads. We plopped into a couple of big, leather chairs and found ourselves charmed and delighted with the atmosphere. It proved to be a nice start to a very pleasant stay.

In the lobby is a huge brown bear, paw offered in welcome. Well, we assume it was welcome. The old guy was stuffed. Nearby was a twelve-foot waterfall that provided all the background sound we needed, and another bear skin was stretched out on the wall.

Just off the lobby is Salmon Run, the main dining room, which offers breakfast, lunch, and dinner. The place is low-key and tasteful. Local kids provide pleasant wait service. The prices were moderate and the menu varied.

Next door, with the same decor, is Black Bear Saloon, and that's where the entertainment is every night. The menu here is more casual.

Continuing on our gustatory tour, Trapper's Outpost offers a variety of fresh-baked goods and pastries as well as salads, sandwiches, gourmet coffee, and soft drinks. It also has a limited selection of t-shirts and sweatshirts featuring the Sawmill logo. The Outpost is adjacent to the pool area, and the food is inexpensive.

Mulligan's Pub serves golfers coming off the ninth green. It offers inexpensive lunch and dinner, and the view over the pond is very pretty. There is also the Tall Pines Sports Bar, which has a bar menu, pool table, video games, and a television locked in to sports programming.

Mariner's Club, on the lake, is part of Mariner's Village Yacht Club. Reservations are suggested; the menu is almost the same as Salmon Run's.

There is also room service, but why anyone would eat in their room despite this variety of choices baffles us.

There is much to do at the Lodge, both indoor and outdoor: basketball, bocce ball, croquet, ping pong, tennis, and volleyball. There is also the fitness center, which has everything it is supposed to have. It's open from 7 A.M. until midnight, and we stuck our heads in just to look around. Spotlessly clean and well-maintained. Of course, we weren't packing on the weight by taking advantage of any of these; still, they're there.

THE LODGE REFLECTS THE ART AND LIFESTYLE OF THE ORIGINAL INHABITANTS, WOODLAND INDIANS

Carriage rides are available, and they are more fun than you might think. The carriage itself is old and large, pulled by a great old dray horse around the beautifully-landscaped grounds. Fifteen bucks for fifteen minutes, twenty bucks for twenty minutes.

The Lodge Beach is north of the golf course, adjacent to the Sheldon Marsh State Nature Preserve—for those of us who love a walk in the woods, this is wonderful.

There are two swimming pools. The Falls, the indoor version, is heated and has a cascading waterfall, whirlpool, and men's and women's saunas. Outdoors is the Olympic pool, open from Memorial Day to Labor Day. On Saturdays, sandwiches are served poolside.

Other services include the Conference Center, which can take care of business or other groups up to 600.

At the entrance to the resort is the 1887 Shops. The name comes from the year the barn was built. Inside are the Men's Shop (Chaps, Nautica, Tommy Bahama, etc.) and the Women's Shop (Joseph Ribcoff, Bon Saken, Joseph A., Sigrid Olsen).

There is a lot of great gift shopping in the barn, and it's fun to walk across the original plank floors under the original beamed ceilings.

While we couldn't find any good reason to leave the resort, the area offers a virtual smorgasbord: Cedar Point is close by, and so is the Huron Playhouse (Ohio's oldest theater—reservations are necessary), the birthplace of Thomas Edison, Firelands Winery, and the legendary Lake Erie Islands.

THE GOLF

This is a Tom Fazio design from 1973. We think it's one of Ohio's great resort courses. The wind is a factor, and director of golf Chris Bleile said the toughest wind is out of the south. That was our wind. Far more playable, he said, is an east-west wind. The greens are big and very fast. Leaving the ball above the hole is often the beginning of a bogey or worse. That lesson was taught on the opening hole; any player above the hole suffered. Nos. 1, 2, and 3 are virtually landlocked, but not without virtue. No. 3 is especially fun with water on both sides of the 150-yard markers. It's a short, 471-yard par 5. This dogleg left wants players to play down the left side.

No. 4, the number one handicap hole, is a tough par 4 of 398 yards. Getting there turns out to be the easy part; this quick green slopes from right to left and again, playing from above the hole is courting trouble.

No. 5 is another notable hole. A par 3 of only 128 yards, the river runs the length of it down the right side. The river then swings around back of the hole, so overshooting is as bad as slicing here. Water has some influence on the rest of the holes on the front.

No. 10, a dry par 4, is long: 408 straightaway yards with probably the best bunker design. Only the number 12 handicap, a par here can clear the books of skins and presses.

Nos. 13 and 14 were memorable holes. The first is a 150-yard par 3, and the shot carries water the whole way. The wind is a factor. Not to be too literary, but the wind in the willows.

We asked aloud, "how many matches have been settled on 18?" It's a great finishing hole, a 437-yard par 4 that calls for a long drive and an approach to a small, elevated green.

Maybe Fazio's genius is in creating courses that are playable, as this one is, but demanding if scoring is important. No one turns in an accidental or lucky score here. If the score is a good one, so is the player.

IF WE SPENT EVERY WEEKEND HERE, WE COULD GET WORK AS SUMO WRESTLERS.

ACCOMMODATIONS

The Lodge at Sawmill Creek Resort   (800) 729-6455
400 Sawmill Creek, Huron, OH

ROOMS: 236; **SUITES:** 48

ROOM RATES: $120–$155   **PAYMENT:** checks, MC, VS, AX, DIS

SPECIAL RATES: AAA

RESTAURANTS: Salmon Run (avg. entree $20), Mulligan's Pub (avg. entree $8), Mariner's Club (avg. entree $21)

RESORT AMENITIES: tennis & volleyball courts, marina, Sawmill Creek shops

CONFERENCE/BUSINESS MEETING FACILITIES: Golf-oriented business meetings are a major part of their business; offer more than 35,000 square feet of facilities and can accommodate up to 2,000.

SPECIAL PROGRAMS FOR CHILDREN: Saturday afternoon pool activities and additional activities on request, Memorial Day through Labor Day

GOLF

GOLF PACKAGE RATES: $329–$619 for 1–2 days and 1–2 rounds

PACKAGE INCLUDES: breakfast for 2, cart rental; weekend packages available; Sun–Thu packages available

COURSE:

Sawmill Creek Golf Course   (800) 729-6455
400 Sawmill Creek, Huron, OH

OTHER ATTRACTIONS NEARBY

Cedar Point Amusement Park, ferry service to Put-In-Bay & Lake Erie Islands, Thomas Edison Museum & Birthplace.

DIRECTIONS

I-90 west; west on SR-2 to Huron (Rye Beach Blvd.); north on Sawmill Creek Rd.; on right.

NORWALK, OH
EAGLE CREEK

*The best ticket for a
"pure golf" getaway*

This getaway is purely for the golf, and it's so close to greater Cleveland we could ride a bike there. We wouldn't, but we could. Less than 60 miles away, it took us less than an hour to get from the West Side to Best Western in Norwalk. It was standard and nice: clean room, pool, Jacuzzi, and lots of channels on the telly. The restaurant of choice in town is Berry's, where we enjoyed an all-American supper: on one side of the table there was fried chicken, mashed 'taters, and creamed corn. On the other side was meatloaf, mashed 'taters, and salad. For dessert we had peach pie and rice pudding.

LOCATION: Northwest OH
DRIVE TIME: 1–2 hours
COST: $$

STAY: Best Western, Norwalk, OH
PLAY: Eagle Creek Golf Club, Norwalk, OH
NEARBY: Cedar Point Amusement Park

THE GOLF

This excellent golf course has an interesting history. Originally known as the Norwalk Country Club when it was built in 1920, it had only nine holes. It went semi-private in 1942 when the Fraternal Order of Elks bought it. It went public in 1973 and was purchased in 1994 by its present owners, who bulldozed the old course, bought two adjacent farms, and created Eagle Creek Golf Club (one of six courses in the U.S. with that name, by the way), a course that is better designed, maintained, and conditioned than some private clubs.

Gary Wilkins, head golf professional, said the goal is to present a beautiful, manicured course that is challenging and appeals to the upper end of the golf market. If those were his goals, we can certainly say that he succeeded.

Brian Huntly designed the new course. He also designed Raintree in Canton, Deer Ridge in Mansfield, and Eagle Landing in Maumee. Superintendent James Baran has a private club background, and it is reflected in the conditioning here.

The driving range and practice green are close to the first tee. The pace of play here is brisk: 4:16 is target time and we finished in 4:05 with no rushing.

There are six pin placements; the starter tells players the placement of the day. There are black-and-white striped marker sticks at the 150-yard mark in every fairway, a design trick we saw at StoneWater GC, and liked very much. Faraway plates are at 100 and 200 yards.

While there is substantial water, we found it more aesthetic than hazardous, a point of contention with Wilkins. There are also wetlands, the hazard from which no ball returns. They border Nos. 11 and 13.

There is an inordinately high number of blind tees: Nos. 2, 3, 10, and 11, and the sand here is fluffy and fun.

The riding carts have armrests and handles built into the roofs to prevent players from toppling out.

For a pure golf getaway, this may be the best ticket: Best Western, Berry's, and 36 a day at Eagle Creek.

ACCOMMODATIONS
....

Best Western   (419) 663-3501
351 Milan Ave., Norwalk, OH

ROOMS: 56; **SUITES:** 5

ROOM RATES: $49–$129   **PAYMENT:** MC, VS, AX, DIS, DC

SPECIAL RATES: AAA, AARP, Gold Crown

RESORT AMENITIES: indoor pool, health club, sauna, hot tub, cable TV/movies, smoking rooms, non-smoking rooms, conference facilities

CONFERENCE/BUSINESS MEETING FACILITIES: can accommodate meetings and seminars

GOLF
....

COURSE:

Eagle Creek Golf Club   (419) 668-8535
Eagle Creek Dr., Norwalk, OH

OTHER ATTRACTIONS NEARBY

Cedar Point Amusement Park, Norwalk Industrial Park, Norwalk Raceway Park

DIRECTIONS

I-480 west; west on I-80 to exit 118/7 for SR-250 (Milan Ave.);
five miles on right next to Hartland Plaza and Pennzoil.

SO CLOSE TO CLEVELAND THAT WE COULD RIDE A BIKE THERE.

OREGON, OH MAUMEE BAY RESORT

An ideal family vacation awaits in, yes, Toledo

LOCATION: Northwest OH	
DRIVE TIME: 1–2 hours	
COST: $$$	

STAY: Maumee Bay Resort, Oregon, OH
PLAY: Maumee Bay Golf Course, Oregon, OH
NEARBY: Cedar Point Amusement Park

This place has a lot going for it: proximity, very good lodging and meals, a fine Arthur Hills–designed course, and first-class activities for families.

The Maumee Bay Resort & Conference Center features a strikingly handsome lodge built a decade ago along with the golf course. The main building has all the stuff it should have for families on vacation: swimming pool, game room, etc. And some that were surprises, such as the small library and comfortable reading chairs.

The resort looks bright and clean-cut, with its many windows, open areas, and the blond woodwork. But then again maybe we got that impression from the herd of kids there on a Lutheran retreat. As far as kids go, Lutherans are right up there on our clean-cut scale. Not as high as Mormons, but who is?

We enjoyed the Waters Edge restaurant and feasted on the all-you-care-to-eat perch. One of us ordered pork chops Diablo. On the dessert menu was apple-brandy brie flambé. We would have ordered it, but we quit smoking two years ago.

We didn't have time to slip into Maumee and dine at the historic Linck Inn, which first went up in 1836, but we won't miss it next trip. The building has been honored by the National Historic Preservation Society. In 1973, the Inn was designated an Ohio Historical Landmark and later listed on the National Register of Historic Places. It has characteristics of Greek Revival and Georgian architecture. Among the characters who enjoyed its hospitality were Abraham Lincoln, Ulysses Grant, and Al Capone. Management doesn't swear they were there, but suggests it. Like our older brother says, when the choice is between fact and legend, always go with legend. Management says the place has ghosts, too.

Another slipaway to consider: the Toledo Mudhens play baseball here. The minor-league franchise likely provides better baseball than the overpaid and overweight Cleveland Indians.

If you enjoy the West Side Market, you'll love a couple hours at the Farmer's Market of Toledo, now in its 168th year. It's in the warehouse district and is al fresco.

The restaurant at the resort has good food, good service, and great views. We told our waitress that the view of the lake, featuring the Davis-Besse nuclear plant, was both gorgeous and unsettling. She said everyone says that.

THE VIEW OF THE LAKE WAS BOTH GORGEOUS AND UNSETTLING

Our room, like many there, had a view of Lake Erie. In the room were coffee makings (and machine) and small refrigerator. Nice to brew a pot in the morning and then sit on the porch, watching the area wake up.

There are four squash courts, indoor and outdoor pools, and a couple of whirlpools. A paved walkway along the lakefront is filled with walkers, cyclists, and rollerbladers. It's easy to see why it's so popular. There's a large, man-made lagoon with beach, picnic shelters, and pavilion with a stage.

In addition to the lodge there are several cottages so popular they are often booked a year in advance. So popular, more are being constructed. They ring the north edge of the golf course, which means teeing off from the porch to a number of holes is definitely doable. A few are duplexes that share a common porch and look perfect for large-family gatherings.

THE GOLF

Many courses call themselves links courses, but finding a true links course in the U.S. is rare. Links courses are notable not for what they have, but for what they don't have—they are without many features. They are often seaside courses and designed more by Mother Nature than any other hand. Americans don't like them or we'd be building them. We don't; we build parkland courses.

Anyway, the Toledo Open has been played on this Arthur Hills design several times. It is known as Toledo's premier public course, and the local U.S. Open qualifier is played here. So it has the proper credentials.

Maumee Bay Golf Course has only two holes without water. Pro Brad Callaway said a guest of the lodge came to play one day. He rented a set of clubs and bought a dozen balls. He returned to the pro shop after a half dozen holes and bought a second dozen. Those got him to No. 12, when he returned for yet another dozen. He lost those between the 12th tee and the 16th hole and quit.

On weekends, carts are required before 3 p.m. The course opens April

Fool's Day and closes on Halloween. There is off-season play, but it's not advertised. It's ten bucks (you read it here first!) to play all day.

Arthur Hills used mounds to define many of the holes here. Used properly, mounds can do more than that; they can sometimes send the errant ball back toward the fairway.

The first hole is only a couple hundred yards from the lodge, good news for those who want to stroll from their room to the tee in soft spikes. Paved cart paths run the length of the course, a decidedly un-links-like feature. The southeast edge of the course is a little scruffy where it backs into residential property. The lots feature mobile homes, a rusted junk car up to its rims in the dirt, several barking dogs, and one sign: "Keep Out of Garden."

No. 3 is a fooler at the tee. The landing area appears overly generous. It isn't. Thanks to a prevailing wind pushes fades into slices and slices into true banana balls. No. 14, the signature hole here, has O.B. left. It's a dogleg right and wraps around a dogleg-shaped pond. Even from the whites, it's a carry of 240 to clear the edge of the pond. We watched one poor soul send four consecutive balls to sleep with the fishes before he gave up.

On No. 16, the ubiquitous mounds find themselves in the middle of the fairway, and on this hole is to be found the greatest concentration of sand bunkers. The home hole, by the way, has nine traps, including one right in front of the shallow green.

We chatted with a father-son pair who said they often play here, but only off-peak; the rest of the time, they said, it plays slowly. Maybe that's because of all the water—sending balls into the drink slows play.

ACCOMMODATIONS

Maumee Bay Resort   (419) 836-1466
1750 Park Road #2, Oregon, OH

ROOMS: 120; **SUITES:** 24

ROOM RATES: $120–320   **PAYMENT:** checks, MC, VS, AX, DIS, DC

SPECIAL RATES: Golden Buckeye, AARP

RESTAURANTS: Water's Edge (avg. entree $15)

RESORT AMENITIES: indoor pool, outdoor pool, health club, sauna, hot tub, cable TV/movies, room service, smoking rooms, non-smoking rooms, conference facilities, racketball courts, 2-mile boardwalk

CONFERENCE/BUSINESS MEETING FACILITIES: eight rooms and more than 7,500 square feet of meeting space in resort interior

SPECIAL PROGRAMS FOR CHILDREN: activity programs daily Memorial Day–Labor Day; weekends only for the rest of the year

GOLF

GOLF PACKAGE RATES: $245–265/person for 2 days and 2 rounds

PACKAGE INCLUDES: food/beverages, cart rental; weekend packages available; Sun–Thu packages available

COURSE:

Maumee Bay Golf Course   (419) 836-1466
1750 Park Rd. 2, Oregon, OH

OTHER ATTRACTIONS NEARBY

Toledo Mud Hens, Toledo Zoo, Toledo Museum of Art, Cedar Point, Put-In-Bay

DIRECTIONS

I-80 west to exit 5 for I-280; north on I-280 to exit 7 for SR-2; east on SR-2; north on North Curtice Rd. to park entrance.

COLUMBUS, OH
NEW ALBANY LINKS

*Especially fun for couples—
even if half of you don't golf*

Four of us went. Two of us played. Two of us shopped. That's one of the benefits of a big-city golf getaway.

LOCATION: Central OH
DRIVE TIME: 2–3 hours
COST: $$

....

STAY: Hilton Columbus, Columbus, OH
PLAY: New Albany Links Golf Course, New Albany, OH
NEARBY: Ohio State University

The Hilton Columbus, inside and outside, amazed us. The front entrance of this gorgeous building is lined with cobblestone. Once inside, we were greeted by luxury and a feeling of calmness, thanks to the decor and service.

All the public spaces here—the lounge, front desk, pool, and exercise room—are spacious, as if the architect's least worry was space.

Not to stray too far from the Royal & Ancient, but the indoor pool here is next to impossible to resist. Separated from the fitness room by a glass wall, the pool (with hot tub) is atrium-like, with a high ceiling and relaxing light levels. Add to that the upholstered furnishings and tall windows, and you turn to your traveling companion and say, "I don't think we're in Kansas any more."

Accustomed to lesser accommodations on our golf travels, we loved having a concierge at our service and a very professional staff trained to anticipate the needs of guests.

Upstairs, our room had more to delight us. It was big, solid, and handsome with all the amenities—fine soaps, big towels, and elegant tile in the bath, plus a few surprises such as great water pressure in the shower (a rarity in hotels, don't you agree?) and a heating element behind the mirror to keep it steam-free while shaving!

Provocative artwork is found throughout the hotel; it has an almost tangible value to guests: we felt special.

In most of these getaways there is shopping, but Easton Town Center is such a shoppers' paradise that the bargain hunters with us were enthralled, delighted, charmed, surprised, inspired, and grateful after spending the better part of a day there.

THE GOLF

Oh, yes, the golf. Well, this wonderful course was designed by Barry Serafin, designer whose recent works include The Links at Echo Springs, Liberty Hills Golf Club, and Chapel Hill Golf Course. All received three stars in *Golf Digest*'s "Places to Play."

Precision and accuracy work well here, beginning with the first hole; a tree stands in the right fairway and an enormous bunker runs down the left. Trouble lurks on virtually every hole—find eight sand bunkers on the beautiful fourth hole; nine of the gritty buggers on No. 17. Creeks and lakes lie in wait throughout the course.

No. 12 was the most memorable hole. A dogleg left with a sizable pond protecting the front left and left side of the green gave us pause. There's more of the wet stuff all the way down the left side of No. 15, where the water and the idea of the water are both hazardous to par, despite the short length of this par 4.

Staying and playing in the short grass has benefits—no blind to the greens, for one. The course sidles in and around an upscale neighborhood, so we tried to curse with only proper nouns. Both No. 9 and No. 18 are great finishing holes.

The clubhouse was still under construction when we were there, but plans called for a 9,500-square-foot building with a banquet room for 80.

ACCOMMODATIONS

Hilton Columbus   (614) 414-5000
3900 Chagrin Dr., Columbus, OH
ROOMS: 313; **SUITES:** 8

ROOM RATES: $149–$219   **PAYMENT:** checks, MC, VS, AX, DIS, DC

SPECIAL RATES: AARP, AAA

RESTAURANTS: The Dining Room

RESORT AMENITIES: indoor pool, health club, cable TV/movies, room service, smoking rooms, non-smoking rooms, conference facilities

CONFERENCE/BUSINESS MEETING FACILITIES: 17 meeting rooms including 10,000-square-foot ballroom; can accommodate 10 to 1,200 people

GOLF

COURSE:

New Albany Links Golf Course   (614) 855-8532
7000 New Albany Links Rd., New Albany, OH

OTHER ATTRACTIONS NEARBY

Easton Town Center (retail shops, dining, entertainment, 30-screen movie theater), Ohio State University, Columbus Museum of Art, COSI

DIRECTIONS

I-71 south to Columbus; east on I-270 to exit 33 for Easton; right on Chagrin Dr.

TROUBLE LURKS ON VIRTUALLY EVERY HOLE; CREEKS AND LAKES LIE IN WAIT THROUGHOUT THE COURSE.

COLUMBUS, OH
THE LOFTS & COOK'S CREEK

Romantic and stylish, this getaway will impress

LOCATION: Central OH
DRIVE TIME: 2–3 hours
COST: $$$

....

STAY: Lofts Hotel & Suites, Columbus, OH
PLAY: Cook's Creek Golf Course, Ashville, OH
NEARBY: downtown Columbus

The Lofts bills itself as "A Hotel With Style." Talk about understatement. The Lofts is the sexiest, hippest, most stylish hotel in the Midwest. Built for a plumbing supply company in 1882, the building is just off High Street, a high, wide, and handsome boulevard.

Taking this building, which is on the National Register of Historic Places, from antique to working hotel called for the imagination of a child, the vision of a preacher, and the gambling instincts of the Maverick brothers, Bret and Bart.

There are only 44 rooms here. We enjoyed a corner suite. With an 18-foot ceiling, we were able to do more than swing a driver; we hit a number of sand shots before leaving to play.

Six windows filled the corner, each five feet wide and twelve feet high. Exposed beams, pipes, and ductwork make the ceiling interesting. Vintage photos of Columbus hang on the walls. The color scheme is elegant: silver and shades of gray. The feather bed—big enough for soccer practice and more comforting than ice cream—elicited smiles. Furnished with rich, pure cotton linens, the bed can sleep six comfortably, ten if they're related.

The Lofts has one of the great bathrooms. It is roomy, elegant, and functional. Honeycombed black and white tiles line the floor; wall tiles salvaged from the New York subway line the walls. The bath is a step up and big enough for two. The personal care products are Aveda.

The Lofts is only a few blocks from Short North, the jazzy art and

restaurant section that stretches for a mile on both sides of High Street. The Short North hosts a gallery hop on the first Saturday of every month.

On the southern end of High Street is German Village, which was originally South Columbus. It's home to one of the world's most enjoyable bookstores, The Book Loft, a 32-room bookstore that gives new depth and meaning to browsing. Few neighborhoods are more amenable to strolling than German Village, with its houses and streets of brick, and it is dotted with wonderful places to stop and eat.

Columbus, of course the home of the Ohio State Buckeyes football team, has expanded its sports offerings, both participatory and spectator. The Columbus Marathon is one of the best in the country, and one reason is the course, which winds through Short North, the OSU campus, German Village, and other neighborhoods before wrapping up at the Ohio Statehouse. It would make a great bike tour, too. The runners kick up their heels in late October.

Triple-A baseball has been here for more than two decades, turning out five dozen players who made it to the bigs, including Derek Jeter, Dwight Gooden, and Andy Pettitte.

When we discovered Columbus has a major league lacrosse team, we

slapped our foreheads and said, "Just how much free time do these people have?" The Columbus Landsharks play a 14-game season from De-
cember through April in Nationwide Arena.

There is also soccer and National League Hockey, and last but not
least, golf. On the OSU campus is the Jack Nicklaus Museum, though
why there would be a museum to some guy who still shoots in the 60s at
Augusta is a mystery. It is Nicklaus's magnificent, if weather-marred,
Memorial Tournament every spring that brings the best players in the
world to Muirfield Village and the course that Jack built.

Columbus is one of the towns we visited for this book that we would
go back to, sans clubs, to enjoy for a long weekend or longer.

THE GOLF

But we came to play. And among the many courses here is one of
America's very good ones, Cook's Creek, just south of town. This young
course (1996) is the pride and joy of a remarkable threesome: designers
Michael Hurdzan and Dana Fry and PGA Tour player John Cook.

Where Hurdzan and Fry go, great courses are left in their wake.

It is a big and rangy course with a lot of great views. Although it appears that water is on every side of every hole, water's role is really more
in shaping holes and making them beautiful than confounding those
who suffer from Terminal Slice. Well, that's for the trunk slammers playing the whites. For the Big Boys, who tee it up from the waybacks and
play all 7,071 yards, the water *can* become hazardous.

Everything on this course is in moderation: trees, sand, water, and resistance to par. It is playable, beautiful, and comfortable. Most landing
areas are generous. As my friend Don Franceski said of the greens, "you
have no business four-putting any of them." Lots of tees are elevated, and
the pace of play is brisk.

EVERYTHING ON THIS COURSE IS IN MODERATION: TREES, SAND, WATER, AND RESISTANCE TO PAR.

ACCOMMODATIONS

Lofts Hotel & Suites   (614) 461-2663
55 E. Nationwide Blvd., Columbus, OH

ROOMS: 44; **SUITES:** 22

ROOM RATES: $199–$139   **PAYMENT:** MC, VS, AX, DIS, DC

SPECIAL RATES: Discounted prices on weekends; breakfast, dinner, and champagne packages

RESTAURANTS: Max & Erma's adjacent (avg. entree $11)

RESORT AMENITIES: indoor pool, fitness center, sauna, cable TV/movies, room service, conference facilities

CONFERENCE/BUSINESS MEETING FACILITIES: meeting space in Lofts and also available in adjacent Crown Plaza Tower

GOLF

COURSE:

Cook's Creek Golf Course   (800) 430-4653
16405 U.S. Rte. 23 South, Ashville, OH

OTHER ATTRACTIONS NEARBY

Arena district (sports, shopping, restaurants, entertainment); Short North (galleries, restaurants, entertainment); German Village; Center of Science and Industry museum; Columbus Museum of Art

DIRECTIONS

I-71 south to Columbus; exit Broad St.; west on Broad; right on High St.; right on Nationwide Blvd.; Lofts shares a driveway with Crown Plaza Tower.

DUBLIN, OH
DUBLIN & DARBY CREEK

A tourist-friendly getaway for art lovers

LOCATION: Central OH
DRIVE TIME: 2–3 hours
COST: $$$

....

STAY: Mariott Dublin Northwest, Dublin, OH
PLAY: Darby Creek Golf Course, Marysville, OH

Dublin, Ohio, bills itself as The Emerald City and adds "steps from Columbus." Trust us, Dublin doesn't need Columbus to be worthy of a getaway trip. This delightful burg offered us wonderful dining, great accommodations, and terrific golf.

Might as well start with the dining, right? No foursome travels well on an empty stomach, after all. The choices in Dublin are many and varied; the quality is high throughout. On our first trip there, we fell in love with Oscar's of Dublin, one of many "casual fine dining" spots there. The menu is all-American, and whoever works the grill there has a deft touch. Steaks, chops, and fish dominate, and we loved the steaks and the pasta. The decor is rustic, and in the summertime, the patio is open and bustling. We found it to be perfect for adults without kids, and we were especially pleased with the service. Someone at Oscar's understands the role played by the wait staff. Another place not to be missed is LaScala Italian Bistro with its handmade pastas with rich red sauce and wood-fired pizza oven.

Five hotels here package golf with a dozen courses, so Dubliners understand better than most the rewards of marketing their city's strengths. No convention and visitors bureau was more responsive to this book; none was more professional.

We stayed at the Columbus Mariott at Tuttle Crossing, which seems oriented toward business-class guests. The guest rooms are large and comfortable, available with two queen-size beds or one king and a fold-out couch. Add an indoor pool, an exercise facility, and an in-room coffee maker, and we were right at home. (I don't know why we say that: we don't have an exercise facility or indoor pool at home. We do have a coffee maker, but it's in the kitchen.) It also had a great breakfast buffet and wonderful staff.

Dublin, which nestles on the banks of the Scioto River, was first settled in 1802. One of several great outdoor sculptures here is the Chief Leatherlips Monument, a 12-foot-high limestone portrait of the Indian killed by his own for refusing to fight white settlers. Dublin's Historic District is worth an entire day of leisurely walking, shopping, dining, learning, and enjoying. The tree-lined streets feature fascinating little shops and taverns, Irish import shops, and coffee bars. We would be remiss if we didn't spend a day taking in the sights and pleasures here, beginning with the

great Art in Public Places. Suddenly art is part of the landscape, and kids as well as adults respond with smiles, raised eyebrows, and thoughtful study. (Take a camera!)

While we're always eager to get to the first tee, a trip to this part of the state ought to include a few hours or more at the Columbus Zoo. It is a home for manatees and 700 species of wildlife. And that's not counting the junior class at Ohio State!

THE GOLF

The twelve golf courses that work with hotels to provide packages are all within twenty minutes of the hotel. Each has its own personality and challenges. Most have driving ranges, food service, and pro shops. Four area courses can be played with the package at no additional cost; others have taken a cue from Myrtle Beach and added surcharges (which is one of a few reasons we don't go to Myrtle Beach any more).

We played Cooks Creek while we were here, but that magnificent track is described elsewhere in this book. We'll only add that this Audubon sanctuary and Blue Heron rookery, bordered by Little Walnut Creek and the Scioto River, is one of the state's finest public courses.

We also played Darby Creek Golf Course, where the front and back nines are fraternal twins and where we were challenged by designer Geoffrey Cornish. Darby Creek can stretch as long as 7,087 yards, but we don't play with people who play from those tees. Even the blues are long here: 6,645 yards. The whites play 6,174 and the reds 5,197.

On the front side, fairway sand is an issue on all the par 4s and 5s, except No. 8, the number two handicap. The sand is replaced with deep water in the elbow of a dogleg right. The back side is more parkland golf and boasts one very challenging finishing hole. No. 18 is 432 yards from the whites, a par 4 whose approach challenges a lot of water on the left and front of the green. It is one of those holes that can make heroes as well as break hearts.

ACCOMMODATIONS

Mariott Dublin Northwest   (614) 791-1000
5605 Blazer Memorial Parkway, Dublin, OH

ROOMS: 303; **SUITES:** 6

ROOM RATES: $129 and up   **PAYMENT:** checks, MC, VS, AX, DIS, DC

SPECIAL RATES: Seniors; AAA; entertainment packages;"Marriott Come Out and Play" rate (summer discount); "Two for Breakfast" package

RESTAURANTS: River City Grille Restaurant and Lounge (avg. entree $8–$15)

RESORT AMENITIES: indoor pool, health club, hot tub, cable TV/movies, room service, pets welcome, smoking rooms, non-smoking rooms, conference facilities

CONFERENCE/BUSINESS MEETING FACILITIES: 12,585 square feet of flexible meeting space with a ballroom that can accommodate up to 700

GOLF

GOLF PACKAGE RATES: $129–$256 for 1–2 days and 2–3 rounds

PACKAGE INCLUDES: cart rental; weekend packages available; Sun–Thu packages available

COURSE:

Darby Creek Golf Course   (937) 349-7491
19300 Orchard Rd., Marysville, OH

OTHER ATTRACTIONS NEARBY

15 minutes from downtown Columbus: Columbus Museum of Art, Center for Science and Industry, German Village, Short North (antiques, galleries, restaurants, entertainment), 3 major shopping areas

DIRECTIONS

71 south to Columbus; west on I-270 to exit 119B; exit 15 for Tuttle Crossing Blvd.; left onto Tuttle Crossing; left onto Blazer Memorial Pkwy.

MT. STERLING, OH
DEER CREEK RESORT

Rustic but elegant, and great for families

LOCATION: Central OH
DRIVE TIME: 2–3 hours
COST: $$

....

STAY: Deer Creek Resort, Mt. Sterling, OH
PLAY: Deer Creek State Park Golf Course, Mt. Sterling, OH

Just to see how much our kids would enjoy being hauled around by their parents and forced to sleep in a cabin, we roped and tied ours and took them to Deer Creek Resort and Conference Center, which is just a half hour south of Columbus.

Ohio state parks have a great many activities for kids and families, and there are some nearby sites we'd like to revisit. Aha! Next year, when Papa Bear goes to Columbus for a couple days, he's taking everyone and making camp at Deer Creek.

While our idea is a great one, it takes a little planning. Deer Creek is not half-filled, waiting for families to show up—the place does a very good trade, so reservations, the earlier the better, are a must.

The lodge here was built in 1981 and still has an open, fresh feel to it. The lobby area is ample and features a huge fireplace (for winter visitors), a charming (Mama Bear's word, not mine) gift shop, and Rafter's, the resort restaurant.

The property, managed by Delaware North Companies, is deep into a renovation and upgrade program. Already the 110 guest rooms have been pleasantly redone, and work is well under way on the 25 cabins.

If your brood is going to take advantage of the amenities here, better you should stay in the lodge. There are indoor and outdoor pools, and near the outdoor pool is access to the lake, a volleyball court, and a putting green. The list of activities offered is a long one that sometimes involves a modest additional cost: crafts, storytelling, hayrides, make-your-own sundaes, etc.

The guestrooms in the lodge's loft feature bunk beds and have small refrigerators, hair dryers, a desk, television with great cable selection, and a nice view of the woods or the pool area. The towels in the bathroom are fluffy terry cloth and are so popular there is a polite and cleverly worded DON'T STEAL THE TOWELS sign on the bathroom door. No room service here.

For rustics, romantics, or the childless, the cabins work very well. Built in groups of three or four, they have views of the water and space out in front for a nightly campfire.

We liked the food as well as the service in Rafter's. Trout almondine was nicely prepared, and the menu listed steaks and chicken, some Italian dishes, and seafood. For the kids, there are some pretty healthy offerings: Pepe's PB&J (we didn't meet Pepe), Grizzled Grilled Cheese, and the always popular Pasghetti. The salad bar is average, and the desserts are magnificent—far too good, by the way, for children. The carrot cake was moist and rich, the Key Lime pie was tart, the Snickers pie was smooth, and the Chocolate Confusion was ... truly decadent. (There are a lot of hiking trails in case you need to balance caloric intake with exercise.) Rafter's doesn't open until 7 A.M., so if eating a good breakfast helps you play better golf, and you have an early tee time, there is a Continental breakfast in the lobby or ham and eggs at the golf course grill.

THE GOLF

As course designer Jack Kidwell said, "It's a good, basic golf course." Kidwell has designed more than one hundred golf courses in Ohio, including Heuston Woods and Punderson. For Deer Creek, he was given $750,000 and 350 acres, though he was not allowed to take the course through the woods: good for groundhogs, state officials must think, bad for golfers.

The course is long from the blue tees at 7,116 yards, but they are rarely played—the whites measure 6,663, which is still a lot of course for the average player; the reds are 5,611, which is about 600 yards longer than necessary for a good red tee course. Hitting it straight pays off here and not just in lower scores. These well-conditioned fairways are a delight to walk.

The rough, while problematic, is no longer that your lawn a few days after moving. The ornamental grasses as 150-yard markers are nice touches, as are the landscaped tee boxes on Nos. 10 and 17, and the quaint covered bridge between the green at No. 5 and the next tee.

There are a lot of sand bunkers here, 52 at last count, and while the traps are maintained well, the sand is not the fluffy stuff that is showing

up at newer courses. There are ten ponds on the course, but if your ball lands in one, you obviously worship Seve Ballesteros' style of play.

The great fun at Deer Creek is at the turn; holes 7 through 11 are pars 5, 3, 5, 5, and 3. It begins at No. 7, a pro-length 473-yard dogleg right that's open on both sides. No. 8 is 161 yards to the middle of the green, but water lurks behind for players who don't know their own strength. Now, No. 9 is a three-shotter for almost every one of us; at 554 yards, it's a real par 5. It is also the number one handicap hole. No. 10, another par 5, is the number three handicap hole and measures 531 yards. At No.11, a par 3 of 166 yards, water and sand wait at greenside.

The course is a couple of miles from the lodge; plan accordingly. We liked the pro shop because it was loaded with great stuff featuring the Ohio State logo on golf gear and clothes.

ACCOMMODATIONS
....

Deer Creek Resort   (740) 869-2020
22300 State Park Rd. #20, Mt. Sterling, OH
ROOMS: 110; **SUITES:** 8
ROOM RATES: $85–$120   **PAYMENT:** checks, MC, VS, AX, DIS, DC

OHIO : CENTRAL

SPECIAL RATES: Golden Buckeye, AARP

RESTAURANTS: Rafter's (avg. entree $16)

RESORT AMENITIES: indoor pool, outdoor pool, sauna, cable TV/movies, smoking rooms, non-smoking rooms, conference facilities, hiking trails, bike rental, basketball and tennis courts, boating, skiing, fishing, game room

CONFERENCE/BUSINESS MEETING FACILITIES: ten meeting rooms that accommodate up to 500 and banquet space for 350

SPECIAL PROGRAMS FOR CHILDREN: children's play area, games, outdoor activities

GOLF

GOLF PACKAGE RATES: $155–$189/person for 2 days and 36 holes rounds

PACKAGE INCLUDES: food/beverages, cart rental; weekend packages available; Sun–Thu packages available

COURSE:

Deer Creek State Park Golf Course   (740) 869-2020
22300 State Park Rd. 20, Mt. Sterling, OH

OTHER ATTRACTIONS NEARBY

Slate Run Living Historical Farm (1880's working farm), Greens Heritage Museum, Tecumseh outdoor drama, antique shopping

DIRECTIONS

I-71 south to exit 84 for London/Mt. Sterling; right on Columbus St.; left on SR-207; left on Cook-Yankeetown Rd.; right on Park Rd.; 3 miles to resort.

NEWARK, OH
CHERRY VALLEY
& LINKS AT
ECHO SPRING

Go for the gardens; go for the golf

LOCATION: Central OH
DRIVE TIME: 2–3 hours
COST: $$$

....

STAY: Cherry Valley Lodge, Newark, OH
PLAY: The Links at Echo Spring, Johnstown, OH
NEARBY: Longaberger Homestead

Cherry Valley Lodge bills itself as "The sophisticated retreat with bed-and-breakfast intimacy." We couldn't say it any better. Located just outside beautiful Granville, home of Denison University, the Lodge is a delight. It rests on 18 acres and offers 200 rooms, including 16 suites with Jacuzzi tubs.

The Lodge's strengths are many: great golf, fine restaurant, swimming pool, and the beautiful town of Denison. But its chief strength might be its commitment to its two gardens: the Gazebo Garden and the Cascade Garden.

The Lodge is the only hotel recognized by the American Association for Botanical Gardens and Arboreta. In addition to golf getaways, offers gardening weekends, gourmet cooking weekends, women-only weekends, and special packages for Memorial Day, the Fourth of July, and Labor Day. Rooms in the two-story building look out on the gardens.

(One of the minor but notable delights is that they provide a pair of thick, white, terry cloth robes in the bath. Stepping out of a hot shower and into such a robe is luxurious. For those who think life would be less without such a robe at home, the lodge will bill you $40 if you take one. We're sure management doesn't want to get into the terry cloth robe business, but we hasten to add that's a very good price.)

The Gazebo Garden surrounds a small lake that features a sloshing, splashing waterfall, benches on which to sit and enjoy the view. A variety of trees and shrubs that offer color from spring through fall: pink flowering cherries, river birches, linden trees, white pines, October glory maples, sweet gum, and finger trees, as well as ornamental grasses, magnolias, and black-eyed Susans.

The Cascade Garden has twin streams cascading into a smaller pond, and this garden showcases trees and shrubs. The wedding arbor is

 tucked away here. This garden is "Mother Nature's portrait in browns and greens," according to the lodge's brochure. A walk through the garden might prove a first introduction to rare specimens such as the three-flower maple and the Turkish hazel. Heirloom varieties such as the winter honeysuckle and beautybush are here as well.

More familiar trees include red bud, black tupelos, vernal witch hazel, Norway spruces, Cornelian cherry dogwood, kousa dogwood, cutleaf alder, and Colorado spruce, among others.

Nearby is Willow Hill Vineyards, where retired dentist Dave Rechsteiner and his wife, Elaine, have been making wine since 1981.

THE GOLF

Before checking in, we played a round at The Links at Echo Spring, just a few miles down pretty country roads. It was designed by Barry Serafin, who is fast gaining a reputation for innovative design, great routing, and greens that give pause, whether chipping on or rolling the ball towards the hole. He had a lot of changes in elevation here and he used them wisely.

No. 1 is a tough driving hole, and the hardwoods creep in on both sides as the green gets closer. Serafin had more than a couple hundred acres to work with here, and he obviously enjoyed himself. No. 3, the first of four par 5s, is a dignified, narrow hole that slowly drifts downhill even as it bends to the left. By this point in the game, it's clear the designer doesn't want to use sand to confuse the issue. The wealth of hardwoods make it difficult enough. We played late in the season, so the long rough might not be typical. Healthy, thick rough a few inches long made finding the ball a challenge at times, and the rough generally punished the player for failing to stay in the fairway. While water is here, it's not in play except for on three holes on the back side, and then it's very much in play. Wetlands, however, are a different story. Wetlands provide physical beauty as well as a costly hazard.

The hole of note on the front side is No. 5, which, at a mere 352 yards from the white tees (411 from the blues), sounds like a pushover. It didn't get number one handicap status by being a pushover. Getting on in regulation only means putting on a slippery and undulating green. Players walking off with double bogeys and worse ruefully shake their heads and ask rhetorically, "What the heck was that?"

The back side is wonderful, especially holes 10 and 18. Each uses a line of lakes almost the length of the hole, threatening players who tend to hook the ball.

Other holes on the back side are not so treacherous. No. 12 is only 315 from the whites (376 from the blues), but getting to the green means passing through guardian hardwoods on both sides and over a deep and shaggy ravine that protects the front of the green. "Open Sesame," is not enough here. A couple great iron shots to this shallow green are called for.

No. 14 is a great short par 4, only 291 and a landing area that could be called generous. But the green is two-tiered: the right side three or four feet steeply higher than the left. If the superintendent had a bad night, you can suffer the consequences with cup placement.

The three finishing holes, a par 4, 3, and 5, all feature water that remind us, "it ain't over 'til it's over." No. 16 is the last of the par 4s and rises as it makes ready to bend sharply around water and wetlands. No. 17 is a handsome par 3 with an intimidating lake to the right. At 164 yards from the whites, and our predisposition for slicing when we're tired, it can be problematic.

And 18—glorious, powerful, long, and challenging 18! It plays 394 yards from the whites and 478 from the blues. The green is tucked left behind water and cattails. It's the number two handicap. It makes heroes as well as breaks hearts. If judgment is lacking on the home hole, and the player goes for the green without sufficient club power, disaster waits patiently . . . in the form of water. Echo Springs is playable and pleasurable, very well maintained, and as time goes on will grow in reputation.

PLAYERS WALK OFF RUEFULLY SHAKING THEIR HEADS AND ASKING "WHAT THE HELL WAS THAT?"

We played a second course, an old and great track whose reputation was made many, many years ago: Granville Golf Course, designed by Donald Ross, the influential Scotsman who designed a few hundred U.S. golf courses during golf's golden age.

About 28,000 rounds are played here every season, and the course record, 65, was shot last year by Lancaster, Ohio golf pro Chris Black.

Greens are small and crowned, and this 1924 design is nothing if not handsome. It is challenging yet playable and offers a view or two that belong on postcards.

On the front side, Nos. 2 and 8 demand lots from the tee: the former stretches 444 yards from the tips, the latter is 434. Both fairways rise to the green, and the green on No. 2 is two-tiered. A stream glides through the second and third holes, but doesn't present much of a hazard.

ACCOMMODATIONS

Cherry Valley Lodge   (740) 788-1200
2299 Cherry Valley Rd., Newark, OH

ROOMS: 200; **SUITES:** 16

ROOM RATES: $136–$240   **PAYMENT:** checks, MC, VS, AX, DIS, DC

RESTAURANTS: Cherry Valley Lodge restaurant (avg. entree $20)

RESORT AMENITIES: indoor pool , outdoor pool, hot tub, cable TV/movies, room service, smoking rooms, non-smoking rooms, babysitting service, conference facilities, fitness room

CONFERENCE/BUSINESS MEETING FACILITIES: meeting space to accommodate groups from 5 to 500 with full-service catering available.

GOLF

GOLF PACKAGE RATES: $250–$275 for 1 day and 2 rounds

PACKAGE INCLUDES: breakfast/brunch for two, cart rental; weekend and Sun–Thu packages available; 5 golf packages to choose from including "The Ultimate Golf Package" (includes custom-made complete set of clubs)

COURSE:

The Links at Echo Spring   (740) 587-1890
5940 Loudon St., Johnstown, OH

OTHER ATTRACTIONS NEARBY

Longaberger Homestead, Dawes Arboretum, Willow Hill Winery, Granville Village

DIRECTIONS

I-71 south; south on SR-13; south on SR-16 to Newark; left on Cherry Valley Rd.; on left.

PERRYSVILLE, OH
MOHICAN &
CHAPEL HILL

Kids welcomed—and kept busy

LOCATION: Central OH
DRIVE TIME: 1–2 hours
COST: $$
....

STAY: Mohican Resort, Perrysville, OH
PLAY: Chapel Hill Golf Course, Mt. Vernon, OH

The Mohican nation was a Native American confederacy of subtribes formerly inhabiting the upper Hudson River valley from Albany south to the Catskill Mountains and north to Lake Champlain.

Today it's an Ohio state park.

It is not yet 30 years old, encompasses 6,000 acres, and is rich in historical, geological, cultural, and natural treasures. The region thrives as a family camping location: 153 campsites, 25 two-bedroom cottages along the Mohican River, canoe liveries, horseback riding, boating, fishing, hiking and bicycle trails, a lot of nearby golf, and the Mohican State Park Resort.

The resort is a 96-room (with balconies) facility with an excellent restaurant. Nearby is Malabar Farms, where Lauren Bacall and Humphrey Bogart were married in 1945. Malabar is the 914-acre creation of the late Pulitzer Prize–winning writer Louis Bromfield. The Big House there has 32 rooms.

The resort offers swimming (both indoor and out), basketball, tennis, and volleyball. There are also billiards, ping-pong, horseshoes, shuffleboard, and a short stack of board games.

The meals we took in the Bromfield Dining Room were excellent. The menu is weighed down with chicken, seafood, pasta, and steaks. The place brags about its ribs, and the Sunday brunch makes going home late seem reasonable. It might also brag about the wonderful view of Pleasant Hill Lake, or the grand fireplace that has a commanding presence in the room.

THE GOLF
. . . .

The resort recommends a number of nearby golf courses. We selected Chapel Hill after talking with other guests. It's only five years old and is spread out on 200 acres that used to house the Mount Vernon Bible College. What, you're going to curse on this course?

It's a 45-minute drive to the course, and if that seems long, the physical beauty of the drive makes it worth it. No interstates. No road rage. Oh, there's the occasional SUV with the driver holding a cell phone tightly to the ear, but that's hard to get away from.

The original college building is at the entrance to the course, and up the hill is the clubhouse, which once saw service as the college chapel.

Nelson Smith and Terry Wells bought the place in 1992, hoping to create an upscale course. Smith was married in the chapel, which later became a pro shop. The course, designed by Barry Serafin, opened in June of 1996.

The range is 300 yards deep and has 15 grass tees. The course has four sets of tees and can play as short as 4,600 yards to as long as 6,950 yards. Instead of black, blue, white, and red tees, it's black, teal, white, and magenta. Teal? Magenta?

The designer took advantage of the terrain; it's gorgeous. The first half dozen holes are open while waiting for the new trees to grow. At No. 7, the course suddenly wakes up. It's a 390-yard par 4 from the whites, a powerful dogleg right. Clearing the dogleg calls for 240 yards off the tee. In addition to sand, there is water on both sides of this narrow green.

Its personality firmly established, the course is a wonderful challenge the rest of the way. At No. 11, trees line the right side and a creek, which later slithers across the fairway, is down the left side. The driving area is tough and tight.

ACCOMMODATIONS

Mohican Resort   (419) 938-5411
1098 Ashland County Rd. 3006, Perrysville, OH

ROOMS: 96

ROOM RATES: $110–$150   **PAYMENT:** checks, MC, VS, AX, DIS, DC

RESTAURANTS: Bromfield Dining Room

RESORT AMENITIES: indoor pool, outdoor pool, sauna, cable TV/movies, smoking rooms, non-smoking rooms, conference facilities

CONFERENCE/BUSINESS MEETING FACILITIES: Eleven conference/meeting areas available

SPECIAL PROGRAMS FOR CHILDREN: during the summer, recreational programs are held daily; live birds of prey show every Saturday evening Apr–Nov; children's playground and child's pool

GOLF

GOLF PACKAGE RATES: starting at $230/person, double occupancy for 2 days and 36 rounds

PACKAGE INCLUDES: food/beverages, cart rental; weekend packages available; Sun–Thu packages available

COURSE:

Chapel Hill Golf Course   (740) 393-3999
7516 Johnstown Rd., Mt. Vernon, OH

OTHER ATTRACTIONS NEARBY

Mohican Fun Center (go karts, water slides, miniature golf); Pleasant Hills Lake (marina, park); canoe liveries; horseback riding; Amish country

DIRECTIONS

I-71 to exit 165, SR 97 East through Bellville and Butler; left on McCurdy Rd.; right on Goon Rd.; left on Ashland County Rd..

CAMBRIDGE, OH
SALT FORK RESORT

*Off the beaten path, but not too quiet,
and lots of wildlife to see*

There were license plates from Virginia, Minnesota, Illinois, Kentucky, and Pennsylvania in the parking lot, a clear indication that this state resort has drawing power. It is off the beaten path—it seemed like we would never arrive after exiting I-77—and has a world-of-its-own air.

LOCATION: Southeast OH
DRIVE TIME: 2–3 hours
COST: $$

STAY: Salt Fork Resort, Cambridge, OH
PLAY: Salt Fork Golf Course, Lore City, OH

True story. As we waited to check in, the clerk asked the guy in front of us if his stay was pleasant. He said "Yes, just as it has been for nearly twenty years." The place has legs!

(One of many delightful surprises here is the amount of wildlife. We saw fawns, their coats still spotted white; lots of heron; and a flock of wild turkey.)

The Lodge is semi-imposing, the only structure of substance in the area. Built with wood beams and high ceilings on one of many hilltops, it's a rugged, comfortable place (remember, it's also a conference center). The Lodge has 148 rooms and an additional 54 cottages.

Rooms in the Lodge are more than adequate; neither spartan nor luxurious—color television, but no HBO. Floor-to-ceiling sliding windows face the swimming pool—the centerpiece as far as kids are concerned. There's lots more for kids right there—volleyball, basketball, etc. But the kids appeared sold on the pool. Especially at night, with the sun down, the moon out, and the underwater lights providing the pool with an ethereal mood. While the lodge surrounds the pool, there is enough room between poolside and bedroom window that the delighted squeals of the kids compete with crickets. And both are pleasant. Salt Fork Lake is nearby, and fishermen are out on small boats, in pursuit of bass, bluegill, and catfish; boat rental is available.

The restaurant is called The Timbers, and for players on the golf package it's an uncomplicated way to eat: the package contains coupons for breakfast and dinner. The service was notably good—with the package, the "service charge" is included; that means your tip has already been taken care of. The cynic in us suspects that referring to it as a "service charge," instead of a "tip," results in the wait staff doing pretty well.

And then the human side of us adds, good for them—it's tough work at a remote location, and they do a very good job.

We recommend the vegetable lasagna, a surprisingly zingy dish that tasted as if your Italian neighbor across the street had made it and brought you a plate of leftovers. The prime rib was a good value as well, and beer and wine are served. The menu, while not extensive, is a good one and has enough salads, beef, and chicken dishes to pretty much please everyone.

THE GOLF

Salt Fork Golf Course was designed by Michael Hurzdan, whose mark is on many area courses, including the new track at The Little Mountain Club in Concord, the Links in Olmsted Falls, and StoneWater GC in Highland Heights.

Given the up and down nature of the terrain, routing appears to be more a matter of what the terrain would allow instead of which way the designer wanted to go.

The course, which measures a short 6,056 yards from the blues, 5,786 from the whites, and 5,241 from the forward tees, plays longer than it looks. Slope is only 110. From high tee ground to low landing area back up to high green is a good way to describe the course.

The challenge is in constantly hitting from uneven lies. That and the rough, aptly named; it is deep enough to hide balls from players, thick enough to stop the ball from tumbling down a hillside, and strong enough to twist the clubhead—that rough and those greens, which move faster than the wait staff. Having said that, we should add that the course, very well maintained and conditioned, is fun to play. And it is dramatic. Now there's a combination: drama and fun.

Why, when we stand on the tee overlooking acres and acres of gorgeous golf course, and, in the distance, the lovely verdant hills, and beyond that, the blue-gray waters of Salt Fork Lake . . . why do we think we're going to hit the ball into the next county?

Well-hit drives take off with all the enthusiasm of a puppy but run out of steam just as fast, and when we get to the ball, we say, "I thought I hit it better than that." Wind can be a factor.

The finishing holes are gorgeous: No. 17 is a 193-yard par 3 over a deep ravine to a deep oval green. Not much room for error here. And from the 18th tee, players can see the clubhouse in the distance.

The up and down nature of Salt Fork is unlike any northeast Ohio course—just the ticket for a golf holiday.

ACCOMMODATIONS

Salt Fork Resort   (740) 439-2751
US Rte. 22 East, Cambridge, OH

ROOMS: 148; **SUITES:** 4

ROOM RATES: $122–$165   **PAYMENT:** checks, MC, VS, AX, DIS, DC

SPECIAL RATES: Golden Buckeye

RESTAURANTS: Timbers (avg. entree $13)

RESORT AMENITIES: indoor pool, outdoor pool, fitness center, hot tub, cable TV/movies, smoking rooms, non-smoking rooms, conference facilities, game room, kids' activity center

CONFERENCE/BUSINESS MEETING FACILITIES: 6,000 square feet of meeting space

SPECIAL PROGRAMS FOR CHILDREN: daily schedule of activities include crafts, nature activities, games, and more (summer only)

GOLF

GOLF PACKAGE RATES: $230–$255 per person based on double occupancy for 2 days and 2 rounds

PACKAGE INCLUDES: food/beverages, cart rental; weekend packages available; Sun–Thu packages available

COURSE:

Salt Fork Golf Course   (740) 432-7185
14755 Cadiz Rd., Lore City, OH

DIRECTIONS

I-77 south to exit 47; east on SR-22 to state park entrance; follow signs to golf course and lodge.

LOGAN, OH
CEDAR FALLS
& BRASS RING

Hilly terrain complements the setting and complicates the golf

LOCATION: Southeast OH
DRIVE TIME: 3–4 hours
COST: $$

....

STAY: Inn at Cedar Falls, Logan, OH
PLAY: Brass Ring Golf Course, Logan, OH
NEARBY: Hocking Hills State Park

Yes, that was us singing "Country Roads" at the tops of our voices, as we slid south to Logan, and the Inn at Cedar Falls, hard by the Hocking Hills National Forest. And we ain't ashamed of it, neither!

This wonderful town of Logan, built where Mother Nature had more fun with hills, trees, caves, and streams than any place else in the state, is a true getaway. No televisions and few cell phones here. A lot of hiking trails, though, and some views of a star-studded sky at night that more than make up for it.

The Inn was started only a decade ago when the owner of a log cabin, current innkeeper Ellen Grinsfeld's dad, wondered aloud if visitors would enjoy the place as much as he did.

They do.

A few additional log cabins were hauled in and tacked on, and the two- to four-person luxury cabins are nestled into hillsides and dip into ravines, offering the best vantage points for students of flora and fauna. A converted barn provides simple but cozy accommodations closer to the main building.

Of course, October is prime time to take in the fall colors in this gently mountainous region of Ohio, so book your stay for this season a year in advance. The Inn, by the way, is open year-round, closing briefly in December for the holidays.

Logan is a quaint and small town that is comfortable wearing a New England jacket and hat. There are plenty of groomed hiking trails and natural wonders at which to marvel in the Hocking Hills State Park. We

dallied at the Logan bookstore/cafe and ice cream parlor/antique store among other shops. Think antiques, festivals, artisans, outlet shopping, and county fairs. But think over and over about antiques. Just a bit west is Lancaster, the birthplace of General Sherman. His home is there still.

Breakfast at the Inn is sumptuous and features homemade granola (there goes that John Denver track in the back of our minds again). And dinner! Fabulous. Simply fabulous. Here's an example: melt-in-your-mouth pork tenderloin with autumn vegetable al denté, followed up by pumpkin crème brûlée.

The Inn is a knock-out, stand-alone getaway, so when golf at the Brass Ring Golf Course is added, it becomes a treasure.

THE GOLF

The Brass Ring course is marked by immense beauty and modest length. Many a first time visitor has looked at the scorecard (5,389 from the whites; 5,861 from the blue tees) and scoffed.

Scoffed? Oh, yes, said member Roger Hinderman, who added that many of them, later humiliated by the demands of Brass Ring, vowed never to return. To which we say, *good*: the hell with them if they don't know a great little course when they see one. All you have to be in order to subdue this short little monster is healthy and blessed with accuracy on the course.

Designer Jack Kidwell routed this one right; he used the hills to create tight, sloping fairways and greens that are small, fast, and well guarded.

It is a fun, fair, and challenging round of golf. The course has a practice range and a pair of practice greens.

Clubhouse facilities are worthy of note. Inside is the dining room, which offers a full dinner menu, and the Brass Ring Lounge, which offers a lunch menu with burgers, wings, and daily specials. Both rooms offer views of the course and surrounding area.

Big Bertha might not work so well here, given the tight demands at the tee boxes and the narrow, tree-lined fairways. Almost every tee box gives pause, and a lot of wildlife visits, too, among them deer, fox, and wild turkey.

The lay of the land is described at the first tee. A short par 5 of 456 yards, the narrow fairway bends uphill and left. The approach is played to a small, elevated green guarded by bunkers in front and a pond in the back right.

The par 3s are difficult. Typical is the 190-yard No. 14, which flies over a ravine to a small, well-bunkered green jammed into the side of the hill like a plate. If there is margin for error here, we didn't see it. We should add that once you're on a green, they slope but don't undulate. We think the designer said, "If they get here in regulation, I want them to have a chance at par."

No. 10 is a short, 350-yard par 4 played almost straight uphill, and the green is another one of these shelves slid into the side of the hill. Not a hole to bump and run, obviously. We could imagine a short approach bouncing all the way back downhill.

It is on the back nine that two great par 5s await, Nos. 13 and 15. The former is a double dogleg left, and the fairway is banked to the left before climbing up the side of a steep hill. The approach takes into account power lines as well as sand and water. The latter par 5 is like an amusement park ride: straight up and then, from one of the highest points on the course, straight down to a green with water back left.

The home hole is a benign downhill par 4 and calls for an iron off the tee and a pitch to the green. The tee is one last wonderful view, and the approach has the clubhouse in the background.

A LOT OF WILDLIFE VISITS, AMONG THEM DEER, FOX, AND WILD TURKEY.

ACCOMMODATIONS

Inn at Cedar Falls   (800) 653-2557
21190 SR 374, Logan, OH

ROOMS: 9; **SUITES:** (cottages/cabins) 10

ROOM RATES: $95–$245   **PAYMENT:** checks, MC, VS

SPECIAL RATES: AAA, Golden Buckeye

RESTAURANTS: Inn's dining room (fixed price 4–5 course meal $28–$35)

RESORT AMENITIES: non-smoking rooms, conference facilities, whirlpool tubs, gas log stoves

CONFERENCE/BUSINESS MEETING FACILITIES: perfect site for small retreats; meeting space accommodates up to 24

SPECIAL PROGRAMS FOR CHILDREN: annual calendar of local events available

GOLF

COURSE:

Brass Ring Golf Course   (740) 385-3806
14405 Country Club Ln., Logan, OH

OTHER ATTRACTIONS NEARBY

Hocking Hills State Park (featuring Old Man's Cave, Cedar Falls, Ash Cave), Lake Logan, Garden Accents, Tecumseh

DIRECTIONS

I-71 south to Columbus; east on I-270 to SR-33 for Lancaster; right on SR-664; left on SR-374; on left.

MARIETTA, OH
MARIETTA & OXBOW

Museum and history lovers find plenty to do while you're on the course

LOCATION: Southeast OH

DRIVE TIME: 2–3 hours

COST: $

STAY: Holiday Inn, Marietta, OH

PLAY: Oxbow Golf & Country Club, Belpre, OH

The history of Marietta is so rich and so fascinating that our next trip will combine Civil War studies, American history, and golf. Maybe in that order.

Marietta, now a mere two centuries old, was a bustling riverboat port as well as the first permanent settlement in the Northwest Territory. Its oldest building, raised in 1788, stands tall today, enclosed in the Campus Martius Museum, which was built over and around the building.

After the Civil War, people moving west picked up deeds here, and the cemetery is filled with Civil War dead.

Andy Benson is the president of the visitor's bureau, as well as manager of the Holiday Inn where we stayed. His walls are filled with awards for scoring well on guest surveys. It's simple, he says of the myriad awards: "Our claim to fame is treating our guests like family." Benson is one of those rare guys who loves his work and loves his town. He is an amateur historian of the first order, and he is a gentleman.

Our room had an ironing board, hair dryer, and coffee maker. Outside the room was a fitness center and swimming pool. The dining room, Memories, had its ribs win the "People's Choice Best Ribs" award at the "Taste of the Valley" festival.

Business meetings do well here. There are four meeting rooms fitting groups as large as 170.

The hotel will handle the golf arrangements. There are a number of courses to enjoy, and recently the Marietta Country Club opened its doors to Holiday Inn guests.

There are eight museums in Marietta: the Historical Model Railroad and Doll Museum is a great one. Trolley Tours shows the highlights of the town while the Driving Tours add more detail. Across the Muskingum River is historic Harmar Village. In town is Main Street, where stores of all sorts are a shopper's paradise. The Becky Thatcher Riverboat is permanently moored here, and in September, Marietta is host to the annual Sternwheeler Festival. Last year it drew 125,000 visitors.

THE GOLF

The course we played was Oxbow Golf & Country Club, which is about twenty miles from Marietta. Farmland in a previous life, it was built in 1974 and owned by George and Lloyd Cowell and Ned Tanner. PGA apprentice Eddie Staats told us, "Not a weekend goes by without players from Cleveland coming down to play."

This championship layout has plenty of water and trees. Some of the greens are tiered, and most of the tee boxes need a little work. The back side plays 300 yards longer than the front, and there are three sets of tees (blues 6,558 yards; whites 6,216; reds 5,036.) It is not an overpowering course and only occasionally penal. The course could use some additional signage, such as yardage markers.

RECENTLY, THE MARIETTA COUNTRY CLUB OPENED ITS DOORS TO HOLIDAY INN GUESTS

A good example of a golf hole that challenges without length is No. 2, a 349-yard par 4 that doglegs to the left. At 170-yards from the tee, a creek cuts across the fairway. Lay up or drive it? No. 5, a 468-yard par 5, has a small lake on the left side of the fairway. It influences the tee shot, and it's the same water that can make life difficult on No. 6, another short par 4.

On the back side, the adventure begins with No. 10, a 575-yard par 5 with a generous landing area. That's the last time generosity is displayed on this hole. Players failing to stay to the right on the second shot find their balls bouncing down slope and into a ravine. For many players, the approach is downhill.

The signature hole on this course is No. 12, a 375-yard par 4 that insists the drive land on the right side. On the left, the terrain falls to a creek. The approach is over the same creek to a small, tiered green. To the right of the green is a ravine; trees are on the left. No. 15 has a great tee: firing out of a chute at a lake that sits in the middle of the fairway about 230 yards out. The green is elevated and slopes back to front.

Going over our scorecard, we couldn't help but feel we could score better. So we played a second time. We were right. It's a tough little course that favors local-knowledge, or as we said, "It's sporting but lethal."

Oxbow is also home to numerous tournaments, including the PGA Sectionals.

ACCOMMODATIONS

Holiday Inn   (740) 374-9660
701 Pike St., Marietta, OH

ROOMS: 109

ROOM RATES: $60–$75   **PAYMENT:** MC, VS, AX, DIS, DC

SPECIAL RATES: kids stay free in parents' room; AAA, AARP, Great Rates, corporate rates

RESTAURANTS: Memories (avg. entree $10)

RESORT AMENITIES: outdoor pool, health club, cable TV/movies, room service, smoking rooms, non-smoking rooms, conference facilities

CONFERENCE/BUSINESS MEETING FACILITIES: three meeting/banquet rooms; can accommodate 2–90; all rooms located on first floor; call for pricing/availability

GOLF

GOLF PACKAGE RATES: Spr/Fall: $154 per person, double occupancy; Jun–Sep: call for rates; 2 night/3 day package for an additional $34/person for 2 days and 2 rounds

PACKAGE INCLUDES: food/beverages, cart rental; weekend packages available; Sun–Thu packages available

COURSE:

Oxbow Golf & Country Club   (740) 423-6771
County Rd. 85, Belpre, OH

OTHER ATTRACTIONS NEARBY

Historical Model Railroad and Doll Museum, historic Harmar Village, Becky Thatcher Riverboat, annual Sternwheeler Festival, trolley tours, shopping

DIRECTIONS

I-77 south to exit 1 for SR-7; left at bottom of ramp; on left.

COLLEGE CORNER, OH HUESTON WOODS RESORT

*For nature lovers,
food lovers, golf lovers*

LOCATION: Southwest OH
DRIVE TIME: 4–5 hours
COST: $$

STAY: Hueston Woods Resort & Conference Center, College Corner, OH
PLAY: Hueston Woods State Park Golf Course, College Center, OH
NEARBY: Paramount King's Island

The trip odometer measured 245 miles from our Lakewood home, and we averaged 50.5 miles driven per hour. That's a high average and reflects two adults who only had to stop once en route. Even a big hiccup in the traffic around Columbus (the state fair was opening that day) didn't slow us much.

Pulling into the parking lot here is dramatic the first time—the resort is a series of huge A-frames, built with thick timber and bolts big as a roll of nickels, and set off with windows that bring the outside in. The resorts have plenty of woodland—at Hueston Woods, there's a 200-acre virgin forest for hiking or communing with Mother Nature. The state park is named for Matthew Hueston, who served in the Indian wars and later became one of the nation's first conservationists.

The lodge bends around Lake Acton, so many of the rooms overlook over the lake. The lake is named for Cloyd Acton, a county legislator who helped the state purchase the property. There is a beach as well as a marina, and behind the lodge is a small dock, which serves as a place to sit, swirl one's feet in the water, and remark about the wildlife. As we sat, a heron fished for supper, a half dozen buzzards circled above, a crow in a nearby tree cawed, and a brace of ducks paddled from the security of the shore to the middle of the big lake.

There is a coffee maker in the room, and the joy of vacation is to be had with coffee on the porch, watching the sun come up and light the lake. The resort has two pools, indoors and out, as well as a game room and small, dark cocktail lounge. While enjoying a late breakfast our last day, we watched six women play shuffleboard next to the pool. It was two teams representing three generations of the same family. Ohio's state park resorts are perfect for family reunions.

Guests turn in at a decent hour, get up at a decent hour, and in between load up on fresh air, great golf, good food, and programs not found elsewhere.

Nature programs are offered here, including Fossil Find (kids will go home with fossils 450 million years old—give or take a millennium or two—that they retrieve from the earth); Slimy, Scaly, Bumpy, which studies native amphibians; and Sharp Talons, a close look the hawks and owls of Ohio. All brought to you by a staff naturalist. Your list of stuff to bring might include bicycles (though they are available to rent if you don't bring your own). Bike trails wend through the woods here—guided tours are offered. For more aggressive kids, there is paintball.

Let's get to the important stuff: food. The Trailblazer Dining Room has much to distinguish it. It is one of the A-frames, this one with a 72-foot-high ceiling, a fireplace big enough to roast a water buffalo in, windows on one side that look out over the pool and the lake, and a huge mural of an Indian graces a wall.

The food is just fine. All-American, I like to say, and here that means lots of Italian and Greek. Greek? The waitress said the chef is Greek. Among the appetizers is tyropita, a cheese pastry. He made a pretty good Greek salad and a very good bowl of beef and barley soup. Also on the menu were Grecian chicken and pork chops, along with grilled trout. My Lisa loves trout, but hates having anything on her plate that still has a head attached, as trout often does. Assured her meal would be decapitated, she ordered. It was not only properly and delicately cooked, it was completely without bones—even those little pesky ones that escape the chef's attention.

Chicken Parmesan, spaghetti and meatballs, chicken Alfredo, seafood pasta, a couple of steaks, as well as a nice selection of sandwiches are all served here. There's a kids menu, too, with pizza, chicken nuggets, grilled cheese, and a chef salad. (Chef salad? For kids? How enlightened.)

There's a nice selection of beers (including their own micro brew, Whistle Stop Ale), wines, and a few champagnes. Service is friendly and professional.

Not everyone will do it this way, but we made our tee time for the middle of the afternoon. The course, we figured, would be less crowded; and anyway, we wanted to 1) sleep in, 2) enjoy coffee and the view of the lake, 3) have breakfast at the Trailblazer, and 4) get into nearby Oxford, home to Miami University.

IT'S A BEAUTIFUL OLD CAMPUS AND THE CITY'S MAIN STREET IS LINED WITH RED BRICK

The trip to Oxford was well worth it. It's a beautiful old campus, and the city's main street is lined with red brick. Coffee houses, bookstores, and restaurants line both sides of the street.

THE GOLF

This Jack Kidwell–design covers a lot of ground, all of it gently rolling. From the whites, Hueston Woods Golf Course measures 6,727 yards, a long course for most of us. From the blues, it stretches to 7,005. The forward tees are 5,176 yards—a manageable length. Yardage markers are minimal—mostly there are only 150-yard markers. While the course is long, it is eminently playable. Trees line the fairways, there is little dense underbrush, and, except for two holes, water is not a factor. Neither is sand. Greens feature six pin positions. The rough is deep enough to give pause, but not so deep as to hide the ball. In the summer season, the greens are somewhat slow. There are as many doglegs on this course as there are in the APL pound, some of them 90-degree. For stalwarts, it's a great walking course, and for nature lovers this course at the height of the fall color must be fabulous.

It is the home course for Miami's team in the Mid-American Conference. A graduate student worked as the starter, and the refreshment cart was driven by a recent graduate.

The opening hole gives a good indication of what is to follow. It is a par 5, a big dogleg right that stretches 517 yards to a slightly elevated green protected by a single sand trap. No. 7 is the second par 5 on the front, this one measuring 536 yards. The tee shot is blind; players should carry the crest of the hill, and then find the fairway rolling up and down like a roller coaster.

On the back side, Nos. 10 and 11 are the number one and number three handicaps. The former is a 421-yard dogleg left with only a couple sand traps, and the latter is a 541-yard par 5 whose twisting design reminds me of a garter snake. Just before the green is a pond.

No. 16 is the signature hole here, a par 3 of 195 yards. Players have to either carry a minimum of 175 yards over water or drop just behind the red tees (where it's a total of 89 yards over water). With traps on both sides, the challenge is more psychological than physical.

All in all, one great value.

ACCOMMODATIONS

Hueston Woods Resort & Conference Center   (513) 664-3500
5201 Lodge Rd., College Corner, OH

ROOMS: 92; **SUITES:** 39

ROOM RATES: $99–$219   **PAYMENT:** MC, VS, AX, DIS, DC

SPECIAL RATES: Golden Buckeye

RESTAURANTS: Trailblazer Dining Room; Johnny Appleseed Lounge

RESORT AMENITIES: indoor pool, outdoor pool, sauna, cable TV/movies, smoking rooms, non-smoking rooms, conference facilities, paintball field, target range, marina, fishing, tennis, basketball, shuffleboard, hayrides, playground, bike rentals

CONFERENCE/BUSINESS MEETING FACILITIES: six meeting rooms totaling 9,220 square feet of meeting space and accommodating groups up to 250. Meeting packages are available.

GOLF

GOLF PACKAGE RATES: $221–$249 for 2 days and 2 rounds

PACKAGE INCLUDES: food/beverages, cart rental; weekend packages available; Sun–Thu packages available

COURSE:

Hueston Woods State Park Golf Course   (513) 664-3500
5201 Lodge Rd., College Center, OH

OTHER ATTRACTIONS NEARBY

Paramount King's Island; Historic Metamora, Indiana; The Dude Ranch; The Beach Waterpark

DIRECTIONS

I-71 south to Columbus; west on I-270; west on I-70 to exit 10 for SR-127; south on SR-127 through Eaton to Camden; west on SR-725; south on SR-732 to park entrance.

FRIENDSHIP, OH
SHAWNEE RESORT

*A resort course for families
to enjoy together*

LOCATION: Southwest OH
DRIVE TIME: 5–6 hours
COST: $$

. . . .

STAY: Shawnee Resort, Friendship, OH
PLAY: Shawnee Golf Course, Friendship, OH
NEARBY: Marietta College

Oh, boy, is this place a family resort or what? While we were trying to catch a little shuteye in our bunk beds (with ladder), the sand man had to compete with doors slamming, conversations, guests walking above us, toilets flushing, and televisions blaring. Soundproofing for our first-floor room apparently was not included in the recent renovation.

There seemed to be more ten-year-old kids here than we've seen in any school yard, and they seemed to be enjoying themselves. While we were miffed trying to go to sleep, it's a delight to see kids with their families, enjoying themselves at a state park.

Shawnee is in the foothills of the Appalachian Mountains, close to the Ohio River. The Shawnee State Forest, so named in 1949, has 63,000 acres. The area was used as a hunting ground by the former inhabitants. It is one of Ohio's most scenic areas, much of it marked by valleys and wooded hills. The rare whorled pogonia and the showy orchids are found among the flora here, and the forest is home to black bears, bobcats, and wild turkeys.

After a four-and-a-half-hour drive, we got on a meandering road nearly two miles long. It led to the top of a hill, where a 50-guestroom lodge sits on the edge of a hill. The decor is Shawnee Indian theme throughout. (The name Shawnee translates to "those who have silver.")

The Tecumseh Lounge is just off the lobby. The name choice is somewhat odd, we thought, given the problem many Native Americans have had with alcohol. It has a nice appetizer menu and a couple of big screen televisions. Beyond the lounge is the dining room, which overlooks the

swimming pool and Turkey Creek Lake. Breakfast, lunch, and dinner are served here. Feel like dining al fresco? There's a veranda that connects the lobby and the restaurant.

Meeting rooms and a large game room are located in the lower level. There is also an exercise room, whirlpool, and indoor pool. Just outside is the huge outdoor pool, along with shuffleboard, miniature golf, and a gazebo that looks out over the lake.

The guest rooms have some nice touches, including an additional sink outside the bath. The balcony is inviting, overlooking as it does the woods filled with oak, hickory, buckeye, black gum, pitch pine, sassafras, and Virginia pine. There is cable television but no coffee maker in the rooms. Coffee is available without charge in the lobby beginning at 7 A.M. In addition to the Lodge, there are 25 cottages that each comfortably sleep up to six persons.

Usually, once we arrive at a resort, we stay put. But here, a side trip to Portsmouth is worthwhile. This great old river town has the Floodwall Murals, more than 2,000 feet of floodwall filled with depictions of local history. Muralist Robert Dafford did the work, and it's fascinating.

THE GOLF

There is no golf professional here, though there is a director of golf. The course was a nine-hole layout when the state bought it in 1980 and added nine more. The course is about nine miles from the Lodge, and shuttle service is offered.

Players can walk here and enjoy it. There are wet and dry hazards, but it's a course that can handle a variety of handicaps. The fairway bunkers on nearly every hole help keep players going in the right direction, and the greens, though not fast, had action enough to preclude anyone saying, "pick it up."

The front side is 3,140 out, par 35. Both the number one and number three handicap holes are long. Number one handicap is No. 7, a 419-yard par 4 with water down the left side and fairway sand. No. 9 is the number three handicap hole as well as the lone par 5 on this side. Not only well trapped, this dogleg right is long at 531 yards.

The back side is 3,267 yards, par 37, with three par 5s totaling 1,505 yards.

This isn't championship golf; this is a course for families to play together and enjoy the game.

ACCOMMODATIONS

Shawnee Resort   (740) 858-6621
4404 B SR 125, Friendship, OH
ROOMS: 50; **SUITES:** 25
ROOM RATES: $90–$125   **PAYMENT:** checks, MC, VS, AX, DIS
SPECIAL RATES: AARP; Golden Buckeye; children under 18 stay free in parents' room
RESTAURANTS: O-HEE-YUH dining room (avg. entree $14)
RESORT AMENITIES: indoor pool, outdoor pool, sauna, hot tub, cable TV/movies, smoking rooms, non-smoking rooms, conference facilities
CONFERENCE/BUSINESS MEETING FACILITIES: various conference/meeting rooms accommodate up to 350 guests; full AV services; customized conference packages available
SPECIAL PROGRAMS FOR CHILDREN: daily activities Memorial Day–Labor Day (pool games, hiking trips, arts & crafts, etc.)

GOLF

GOLF PACKAGE RATES: $229–$259/person, double occupancy for 2 days and 2 rounds
PACKAGE INCLUDES: food/beverages, cart rental; weekend packages available; Sun–Thu packages available

COURSE:
Shawnee Golf Course   (740) 858-6621
4404 B SR 125, Friendship, OH

OTHER ATTRACTIONS NEARBY

Marietta College, Fenton Art Glass, antique shopping

DIRECTIONS

I-71 South to Columbus; south on I-270; south on US-23 to Portsmouth; west on US-52; west on SR-125; entrance off SR-125 about 6 miles from US-52.

HAMILTON, OH HAMILTONIAN & SHAKER RUN

Set aside some time to tour this wonderful "City of Sculpture"

LOCATION: Southwest OH

DRIVE TIME: 4–5 hours

COST: $$

....

STAY: Hamiltonian Hotel, Hamilton, OH

PLAY: Shaker Run Golf Course, Lebanon, OH
Walden Ponds Golf Course, Indian Springs, OH

NEARBY: Miami University

Dean Kink, the general manager at the Hamiltonian Hotel, is a veteran of the hospitality industry. With this place, he just nailed a trifecta: the best business and meeting hotel in the area, a kitchen and dining room renowned for its Sunday brunch, and headquarters for golfers eager to test a couple of the best courses in the Midwest.

The Hamiltonian is not a resort, but it's a well-run, functional establishment with clean, well-appointed rooms, a friendly and professional staff, and wonderful food and beverage service.

For added pampering, the sixth floor is the executive level, offering the little things that mean a lot: daily newspaper, a breakfast without charge, two phones with data ports, full length mirrors, and a small gathering area for a few guests to relax.

Next time we go (and it will be this season), we'll plan a bit more carefully. The Sunday brunch is worthy of all the accolades rained upon it. And we think the best way to enjoy it is to get the earliest tee time we can and after 18 glorious holes, shower and make it to the brunch.

The hotel is at Main Street and the Miami River in downtown Hamilton. That puts it right between Dayton and Cincinnati. You don't have to go far for history; just across the street the remnants of Fort Hamilton (1791) wait to remind guests this country wasn't always interstates and fast food. There is a moving firefighters monument there, and the art deco styling of the Butler County Court House gave us pause.

Hamilton sometimes bills itself as the City of Sculpture, probably to brag about its Pyramid Hill Sculpture Park, which has what's left of a 265-acre hardwood forest. It features a 180-year-old stone pioneer home as well as more than 30 pieces of sculpture. An afternoon there is more than interesting; it is thought-provoking, often surreal, often moving—it can be mesmerizing.

We all know (don't we?) about the *McGuffey Reader*; did you know that William Holmes McGuffey and his wife built a two-story brick home in nearby Oxford and lived there while the old man was a professor of ancient languages and moral philosophy at Miami University? The house is a National Historic Landmark and is a fascinating tour.

If it's houses and homes that catch your attention, don't miss the Lane-Hooven House on North Third Street in Hamilton. Talk about limited editions—only 400 of these octagonal houses were built in the U.S., and not very many of them were built, as this one was, of brick. It's in Hamilton's German Village District and is listed on the National Register of Historic Places.

Butler County has its own MetroParks system, and among the historic sites it maintains is Indian Creek Pioneer Church & Burial Ground. It's a nice place to visit and learn, especially if you have a couple kids with you. Given the right opportunity, kids seem to enjoy visiting and learning at places such as this. There is no pressure to learn, only the fun of learning.

For its many delights, Hamilton isn't batting 1.000. It is home to *The Hamilton Gateway*, a piece of public sculpture that will make northeast Ohioans feel less embarrassed by *Portal* and *Free Stamp* and that flying straight razor on East Ninth Street and Euclid Avenue. The Hamilton Gateway is so weird-looking, the brochure that tries to explain it is six pages long. On the back page is a picture of the two people who donated the loot for it, John and Shirley Moser. I notice the artists are in the picture, too, but their names are not revealed. Doubtless to protect the innocent. So if you take the troops to see it, don't laugh; the emperor loved his new clothes, you might recall.

You know the Wright-Patterson Air Force Base is close by, don't you? It's worthy of a few hours. You'll be glad you went; you'll understand a great deal more about the role assumed by air power in war as well as peace. We won't give away all its secrets, but will tell you this: a trip through the Air Power Gallery is as exciting as gunfire.

IT'S A NICE PLACE TO VISIT AND LEARN, ESPECIALLY IF YOU HAVE A COUPLE OF KIDS WITH YOU.

THE GOLF

Shaker Run is considered by many to be the finest public golf course in a state that is blessed with dozens of great ones. Shaker Run is 27 holes; the Woodlands/Lake course was designed by Arthur Hills, and the third nine, the Meadows, was designed by the Hurdzan-Fry team.

How good is this place? The USGA is coming here in 2005 (also the Greater Cincinnati Golf Association's 100th anniversary) with the U.S. Amateur. The winner goes to play in the Master's. Shaker Run received 4½ stars from *Golf Digest*.

We played the Woodlands and Lakeside nines; next trip we'll get in the Meadows.

The 18 we played measured 3,270 from the blues, par 72; course rating was 71.2 and slope was 132 (yow!). We'll say it was more course than we were golfers, but we're not sharing our scores. The joy of playing here for the first time is not in the score, but in the physical beauty of this magnificent track. (How's that for an excuse?) While the global positioning system on the carts is a help, nothing works here as well as a confident swing.

SHAKER RUN GOT 4½ STARS FROM *GOLF DIGEST*

The Woodlands starts with a wonderful warm-up hole, a par 5 of 535 yards, a lot of it gently downhill. It's No. 3 that tests golf judgment as well as golfing skills. The starter told us about this hole and we wisely took a ride down the fairway to get a better feel for the hole before teeing it up. A par 4 of only 385 yards, this number two handicap features what appears to be a small, sunken green protected by a creek in front. Two very good shots will do it, but both have to be good. The greens here roll well and true.

This nine's signature hole comes up at the 5th tee. A par 3 of 190 yards, the first 160 yards tumble downhill, and there is water front and left of the green. This is one of those holes where you don't want to have honors. The wind is as much a part of this hole as the water or the green.

The Lakeside nine is equally delightful. No. 2, a brief par 3 of 135 yards is a tester. There's more room for error in your swimsuit than there is on this hole that begins at an elevated tee box. There is water in front and sand behind the green.

It's the three finishing holes here that have atheists converting and Republicans being kind. These are the holes that make heroes of the unassuming, fools of the braggarts, and loyalists of all manner of players to the Magnificent Triumvirate of Shaker Run, as we called it when we finished.

Nos. 7, 8, and 9 are: 380-yard par 4; 470-yard par 5; 380-yard par 4. Accuracy is a virtue off the tee on No. 7, and the back and right of the green slope to the water. Sand adds a nice diversion in front of the green. No. 8 is a par 5, downhill and a dogleg. What else could you enjoy here?

Oh, yeah! The green, which we thought was smaller than our garage floor, is elbow-to-rib with a ball-swallowing lake.

Shaker Run is one of those rare courses where, about halfway through the 17th hole, players are overcome with sadness. They suddenly realize the match is coming to an end, and there is only one more hole until next time.

We also drove 10 minutes from the hotel to play Walden Pond, in Indian Springs, where the clubhouse, a wonderful brick and stone manse, was built in 1831. The course opened 166 years later. As they like to say there, "perfection takes time."

This is another Michael Hurdzan design, and though water is an important element, it is as much for beauty as it is for adding challenge.

Going out, it's 3,161 yards from the blue tees; 3,243 coming in. That course, 6,404 yards, par 72, is a challenge to anyone unused to that length. Discretion is part of course management, you know. There are six pin positions on the greens.

It begins with a 427-yard par 4 down a fairway with a lot of sand on the sides and ends at a green that is backed up with water. Nothing wrong with getting on in three, we told ourselves as we chipped. No. 4, a handsome par 5 of 528 yards, is a true three-shotter for us and hookers are not allowed here; lots of water down the left side.

No. 10 is one of the area's great par 5s thanks to the water in front of the green. It plays every bit of 497 yards and again . . . discretion.

Michael Hurdzan's trademark seems to be his innate ability to make every hole singular. It makes his courses a delight to play and reminds us how important great design can be.

ACCOMMODATIONS

Hamiltonian Hotel   (513) 896-6200
1 Riverfront Plaza, Hamilton, OH

ROOMS: 120; **SUITES:** 4

ROOM RATES: $85–$120   **PAYMENT:** MC, VS, AX, DIS, DC

SPECIAL RATES: AAA, seniors

RESTAURANTS: Hamiltonian Hotel restaurant

RESORT AMENITIES: outdoor pool, health club, cable TV/movies, room service, pets welcome, smoking rooms, non-smoking rooms, conference facilities

CONFERENCE/BUSINESS MEETING FACILITIES: meeting rooms accommodate 4 to 400

GOLF

GOLF PACKAGE RATES: $200 per person for 1 day and 2 rounds

PACKAGE INCLUDES: cart rental; weekend and Sun–Thu packages available

COURSES:

Shaker Run Golf Course   (800) 721-0007
4361 Greentree Rd., Lebanon, OH
Walden Ponds Golf Course   (513) 573-9993
SR 4 and Walden Pond, Indian Springs, OH

OTHER ATTRACTIONS NEARBY

Soldiers, Sailors & Pioneers Monument, Jungle Jim's International Market, German Village, historic Dayton Lane, Miami University

DIRECTIONS

I-71 south to Columbus; west on I-270; west on I-70; south on I-75 to SR-129, on right.

KING'S ISLAND, OH
KING'S ISLAND

*Drop the non-golfers off at
King's Island and go play where
golf's greatest play*

LOCATION: Southwest OH
DRIVE TIME: 4–5 hours
COST: $$
. . . .
STAY: Holiday Inn Express, King's
Island, OH
PLAY: Golf Center at King's Island,
Mason, OH
NEARBY: Paramount King's Island

While there are no golf packages to be had with the Golf Center at Kings Island, in Mason, Ohio, there are other benefits. Dropping the kids off at the amusement park comes to mind almost immediately. And cruising a Jack Nicklaus course that is playable and accessible is another.

The Holiday Inn Express we stayed at was just right. Nice rooms, crisp sheets, and a reasonable price. Forget something? What? Razor? Shampoo? Toothpaste? Ask at the front desk, and it shall be given to you.

There's no restaurant. In many instances, a hotel restaurant is a drag on profits more than a benefit to guests. Especially if there are a lot of competing restaurants circling the place. That's the way it was here, so for dinner, we took a brief stroll and plowed into plates of a local favorite: 5-way Skyline Chili.

THE GOLF

The head pro at the Golf Center is Andy Horn, PGA, who grew up in nearby Middleton and prepped with Arnold Palmer. He spent seven years working with the King at Bay Hill, and Horn's reminiscences, anecdotes, and observations are delightful. Too bad he doesn't have time to sit with all his guests and enjoy golf talk over a pitcher of beer (only $7 at happy hour).

Horn worked at Bay Hill so that he could play the mini-tours at the same time. But after a decade in the minors, he realized he would have to get a real job. And here he is, proud papa of a very good juniors program as well as a highly regarded teacher.

He is the steward for a long season and an incredible amount of golf: 85,000 rounds. "If the weather is decent," he said, "the people will be here. And the grounds crew is phenomenal." Well south of Columbus, the winters here are relatively brief and somewhat mild. Many northern Ohioans and a lot of Michiganders come to sneak in extra rounds.

This is the course to play if playing where golf's greatest play is important to you. The PGA, LPGA, and Senior PGA Tours have all been here a bunch of times.

There are three nines, and the signatures hole on each is No. 9, especially on the West Course, which, after gliding through a very nice housing development, presents a 526-yard par 5—decidedly a three-shotter for the overwhelming majority. A pond in front of the green gives even the biggest bruisers pause.

The greens are big, subtle, and seductive. They're not especially fast, but we penciled in more three-putt greens here than any other course on this tour.

The condition of this gently rolling layout, no surprise, is quite good, and the driving range and 10,000-square-foot practice green offer a comfortable opportunity to warm up before play.

The championship course is The Grizzly, and for tournament players, it's 6,618 yards, par 72. For the rest of us, it shrinks to a more playable 6,138.

Our Dream Getaway is to arrive with tickets to the Saturday and Sunday play of any of the tournaments, and on the Monday after tee it up our own selves.

ACCOMMODATIONS

Holiday Inn Express   (800) 227-7100
5589 Kings Mills Rd., King's Island, OH

ROOMS: 194; **SUITES:** 1

ROOM RATES: $85–$120   **PAYMENT:** MC, VS, AX, DIS, DC

RESTAURANTS: No restaurant on premises

RESORT AMENITIES: outdoor pool, health club, cable TV/movies, pets welcome, smoking room, non-smoking rooms, conference facilities

CONFERENCE/BUSINESS MEETING FACILITIES: meeting and conference rooms accommodating up to 300 people

SPECIAL PROGRAMS FOR CHILDREN: discounted tickets to Paramount's King's Island and The Beach Waterpark

GOLF

COURSE:

Golf Center at King's Island   (513) 398-5200
6042 Fairway Dr., Mason, OH

OTHER ATTRACTIONS NEARBY

Paramount King's Island, The Beach Waterpark

DIRECTIONS

I-90 west; north on I-75 to exit 29 (SR-63); left on SR-63; south on SR-741; left at King's Mills Rd.; on right.

THE LPA, LPGA, AND SENIOR PGA TOURS HAVE ALL BEEN HERE A BUNCH OF TIMES.

WILMINGTON, OH
MAJESTIC SPRINGS

*For peace and quiet and
some pretty serious golf*

LOCATION: Southwest OH
DRIVE TIME: 3–4 hours
COST: $$

....

STAY: Amerihost Inn, Wilmington, OH
PLAY: Majestic Springs Golf Course,
Wilmington, OH
NEARBY: Wilmington College

Wilmington is Clinton County's county seat, and its downtown, with its signature courthouse, is as handsome as an Amish-made oak dresser. Just an hour south of Columbus, this is Midwest farmland with gently rolling hills. It's peaceful here. Peaceful and quiet.

It isn't Las Vegas, and it isn't New Orleans. It's Wilmington, so the festivals and fairs here are the Clinton County Fair, the Corn Festival, the Banana Split Festival, and the annual Oktoberfest.

Wilmington is home to Wilmington College, a Quaker school. Founded in 1870 by the Religious Order of Friends, Wilmington College maintains the largest repository of materials (outside Japan) on the atomic bombs that were dropped on Hiroshima and Nagasaki.

We stayed at the Amerihost hotel, which has no restaurant but serves up a complimentary Continental breakfast.

We talked about Continental breakfasts that morning over cold cereal, muffins, coffee, and fresh fruit. No other hotel feature saves money and time like a Continental breakfast. Think about it: two guys at $7 each for breakfast, plus tip, and you've not only gutted a $20 bill, but you **WILMINGTON IS AS HANDSOME AS AN AMISH-MADE OAK DRESSER** took nearly an hour to do it, right? (And not to get personal, but if your gut had its choice of bacon fat and runny eggs or a bran muffin and an apple, which do you think would it take?)

With this free service, you not only enjoy a healthier breakfast but you finish in half the time, and there is no bill.

The rooms here are very nicely appointed, comfortably furnished, and include such amenities as a microwave, refrigerator, coffee machine, and data port. We noticed there were more lights in this room than in any other we visited while researching this book. Where do you want to sit? There's a light for you. Five of the rooms here have whirlpool baths.

THE GOLF

We left Amerihost and followed directions to Todds Fork Road, but after a few minutes, we doubted we took the correct turn. The road weaved snakelike through the countryside, and the longer we stayed on it, the less we saw of civilization. Was that the theme of *Deliverance* in the background?

Coming around one bend in the road, we found ourselves just where we wanted to be: at Majestic Springs Golf Course, which, just a couple years ago, was a farm. The course was not quite finished when we played—there were a lot of hazards cut but not yet filled with sand (which made us wish grass bunkers were in the plans).

You were wondering, weren't you, where the name came from? Some beer joint. True. Roger McKay was with friends one night in a local bar and he had a short list of possible names. Champagne Springs was one that didn't make it. Dutch Creek was another. (Dutch Creek is on the property.) "A buddy said, 'Majestic Springs,' and I thought it wasn't too bad," McKay said. When he took the short list to each of the two and a half dozen patrons there, and asked which course they would most like to play. Every single person said, "Majestic Springs."

The course will be more beautiful this season than it was last. And next year it will be more beautiful yet. The course has more potential than any Triple-A ballplayer. Great rolling terrain, enough water to be hazardous, and routing that darts in and out of the woods, up and down hills, over creeks and ponds, and across meadows.

Cows were still grazing when work started in the summer of 1997. Two years later, the first nine holes were opened. There are four sets of tees, and the yardage is deceptive. The whites play only 5,800 yards. A closer look at the scorecard explains: three par 3s on the front side. And the course explains even more: yardage is the way the crow flies, not the way the Dunlop dribbles and bounces. The championship tees are 6,500 magnificent yards. Par 71.

A lot of holes here have tees that give pause. And a number of holes qualify for signature status. No. 11 is a 522-yard par 5, a dogleg left with water all the way down the left side. And No. 15, another par 5, looks like the setting of the Headless Horseman's ride: downhill and through the woods until, 521 yards from the tee box, the fairway meets the green.

Roger McKay says of his brand-new course, "We want everyone who plays here to think seriously about coming back."

We're thinking seriously.

ACCOMMODATIONS

Amerihost Inn   (937) 383-3950
201 Carrie Dr., Wilmington, OH

ROOMS: 61; **SUITES:** 5

ROOM RATES: $63–$175   **PAYMENT:** MC, VS, DIS, DC

SPECIAL RATES: children under 12 free, AAA, AARP, group rates

RESORT AMENITIES: indoor pool, sauna, hot tub, cable TV/movies, smoking rooms, non-smoking rooms, conference facilities

CONFERENCE/BUSINESS MEETING FACILITIES: meeting room accommodating up to 35

GOLF

COURSE:

Majestic Springs Golf Course   (937) 383-1474
1631 Todd's Fork Rd., Wilmington, OH

OTHER ATTRACTIONS NEARBY

Caesars Creek State Park, Cowan Lake State Park, Wilmington College, antique and outlet shopping

DIRECTIONS

I-71 south to exit 50; south on SR-68 to Wilmington; left on 73E; left on Carrie Dr.

THE COURSE HAS MORE PO-TENTIAL THAN ANY TRIPLE-A BALLPLAYER

OTHER
STATES

ANN ARBOR, MI
WEBER'S INN & REDDEMAN FARMS

*Something for everyone
in this historic college town*

LOCATION: Southeast MI	
DRIVE TIME: 3–4 hours	
COST: $$	

STAY: Weber's Inn, Ann Arbor, MI

PLAY: Reddeman Farms Golf Club, Chelsea, MI

NEARBY: University of Michigan

The first time we stayed overnight in Ann Arbor was just a few years ago. Downtown is a delight, jammed with owner-operated stores and restaurants and wonderful, special bookstores. It is nationally known for its nightlife and its devotion to the arts. What made it so special to us was the laid-back atmosphere. Why, it bordered on friendly, and how often do you see that these days?

The historic University of Michigan campus dominates the area, which also offers museums, art galleries, movie houses, theaters, music venues, and a lot of shopping. For the kids, there is a vibrant system of parks across the county and along the rivers—for swimming, boating, and hiking. Kids and parents will both like the Ann Arbor Hands-On Museum, with more than 250 interactive exhibits. Visitors can see a working bee hive, make a hot air balloon take flight, or encase themselves in a giant soap bubble.

While the ride to Ann Arbor is not as exciting as, say, raking leaves, Ann Arbor is one of the Midwest's best small towns.

When one first approaches Weber's Inn, it looks spread out and disorganized. Maybe that's because it began as a restaurant in 1937, moved to its present location in 1962, and added hotel rooms in 1970. A mom-and-pop operation during its Depression origins, it is still run by the Weber family. Upon closer inspection, Weber's is roomy and attractive, with plenty of free parking.

Our second-floor room overlooked the appealing indoor court-

yard/pool area. Outside our back door, a charming spiral staircase led us down to what Weber's calls their "Four Seasons Recreation Area." Six other staircases add atmosphere and connect at least fifty rooms on four floors to the area, which is a kid-magnet by day and by night a great place for a romantic swim, stroll, or snack. Included are ping-pong, billiards, a whirlpool, a sauna, a fitness room, and the Cabana Cafe for light meals.

Our room was comfortable and appealing, with a queen bed and better-than-average motel furniture. Included were some thoughtful amenities, such as a hair dryer, an iron and board, and a safe you can program with your own combination. The TV included Showtime, ESPN, Nickelodeon, and Canadian TV.

The wake-up call was right on time, and *USA Today* was delivered to our door. One quibble: no in-room coffee maker. Newspaper without coffee? That's bacon without eggs, Hansel without Gretel, and hockey without sucker punches. This is why we pack a percolator when we hit the road. Not a coffee maker, which likely couldn't survive the trip, but an old-fashioned percolator. The quality of the brew will surprise you; the convenience will delight you.

ANN ARBOR IS KNOWN FOR ITS NIGHTLIFE AND ITS DEVOTION TO THE ARTS

Like the Inn, Weber's Restaurant defies architectural description. Above a wall mural depicting orchards are large sculptures of various fruits perched precariously on the rafters. With cherry wood tables, stained glass windows, and menu boards in the shape of fish ... we believe the word is "eclectic."

We asked Kyle, our waiter, what was the deal with the colossal cornucopia. Unable to articulate a theme, he merely said that an artist came in one day, and this is what resulted. From across the restaurant, it seemed the couple under the giant apple would have the worst of it in the event of a seismic episode.

Tilapia, a mild freshwater catch, arrived with a flavorful, cheesy breading. We also had the northern lake whitefish, which comes in several interesting presentations, including oven-broiled, pan-fried, and Chef Jerry's "grilled sweet potato encrusted." Each dish was accompanied by rice, a tasty smoked salmon pâté, and a somewhat neglected garden vegetable. For dessert we shared a decadent slice of chocolate cheesecake, for which—along with its prime rib—Weber's claims national recognition. Cool tunes from a nearby piano player added atmosphere.

Strolling back to our room, we noticed that the adjacent Habitat Lounge has nightly entertainment and was about three-fourths occupied with a casually dressed mix of locals and travelers.

The next morning's continental breakfast was complete and nutritious (including fresh fruit), but disappeared quickly.

THE GOLF

A dairy farm until 1990, Reddeman Farms Golf Club is a challenging course that is also easily walkable. The front nine is open and flat; the back nine is wooded and rolling. Ponds and creeks come into play on 13 holes.

While loudly honking geese can occasionally spoil a shot, we all know the real reason to keep geese and golf separate: ubiquitous piles of doo-doo. Patty McCarthy, co-owner of Reddeman Farms, seems to have solved the problem. Mocha, Duffy, and Hogan are her three Labrador hunters that keep the geese at bay. Once, one of the foolish fowls challenged the pooch pack and took possession of a pond; Mocha dog-paddled out to the intruder. After a racket of barking and honking, the chocolate-colored canine swam back clutching his trophy. We saw no geese the day we were there.

Fairways and rough were nicely maintained and well-conditioned. Both range and putting green are available for warm-ups and practice.

The clubhouse restaurant is quite attractive, with reasonable prices and an impressive selection that includes healthy choices such as veggie burgers. Ann Arbor office workers often drive the ten or so miles here to have a quiet lunch in the country.

McCarthy says that her course is a peaceful contrast to the hustle-bustle of the Detroit–Ann Arbor urban corridor. When she gets out on the course herself, and away from the phones, she calls it "the closest place to heaven I know." She seems genuinely interested in providing a pleasurable experience for her customers.

The first hole is a nice warm-up, a par 4 of only 376 yards from the whites, a soft dogleg to the right. To the right of the fairway is a pond, often visited by players who refuse to learn how to control their slices. No. 2 is similar but bends to the right. There is a pond on the right here, as well, to further infuriate those dullards who refuse to take care of that slice. With a barn and a storage shed between tee and green, the adventurous—not to say foolish—launch balls and pray for them to clear the buildings. The pock-marked sides of the building suggest judgment is not one of the many virtues of players here.

Llamas on No. 8. True. This par 5 of only 464 yards has water going down the left side and a pond on the right. Beyond the creek is a farm with llamas, roosters, and donkeys.

The number one handicap hole is No. 9, a 413-yard par 4 that calls for an approach over water. The scorecard notes players finishing the front side should be walking off in two hours, fifteen minutes.

On the back nine, No. 13, a par 4 measuring only 366 yards, is the first of four holes that slip into the woods. While it is short, trouble lies in wait on this dogleg left: water on the left is easily reached from the tee.

The home hole is a very pretty finishing hole, a reminder that natural beauty plays a vital role in golf. Some players are going to get on in two, but this par 5 of 491 yards insists the approach carry substantial water.

Ah, risk and reward at the 18th hole! Sounds like an Agatha Christie novel.

THE ADVENTUROUS LAUNCH BALLS AND PRAY FOR THEM TO CLEAR THE BUILDINGS.

ACCOMMODATIONS

Weber's Inn   (734) 769-2500
3050 Jackson Rd., Ann Arbor, MI
ROOMS: 158; **SUITES:** 10
ROOM RATES: $110–$135   **PAYMENT:** checks, MC, VS, AX, DIS, DC
SPECIAL RATES: AAA and AARP: 10% discount
RESTAURANTS: Weber's Restaurant (avg. entree $16), Habitat Lounge
RESORT AMENITIES: indoor pool, health club, sauna, hot tub, cable TV/movies, room service, smoking rooms, non-smoking rooms, babysitting service, conference facilities
CONFERENCE/BUSINESS MEETING FACILITIES: more than 9,300 square feet of conference space and can host events ranging from conferences to seminars to retreats.

GOLF

GOLF PACKAGE RATES: $157–$170/person; $192–$210/couple for 1 day and 1 round
PACKAGE INCLUDES: food/beverages, cart rental

COURSE:

Reddeman Farms Golf Club   (734) 475-3020
555 Dancer Rd., Chelsea, MI

OTHER ATTRACTIONS NEARBY

Ann Arbor Hands-On Museum, UM Museum of Art, UM Museum of Natural History, UM Botanical Gardens, Ypsilanti Automotive Heritage Collection, Purple Rose Theater, Hill Auditorium, Power Center for Performing Arts, Chelsea Milling, antiques shopping, many festivals

DIRECTIONS

I-80 west to (I-475)/(US-23)/59 exit; south on US-20; right on W. Dussel Dr.; north on I-475/US-23 to Ann Arbor; west on I-94 to Chicago; exit #72 for Jackson Ave.; left on Jackson; right on Jackson Rd.

BATTLE CREEK, MI
GULL LAKE VIEW

*A good place to get away
without the kids*

LOCATION: Southern MI	
DRIVE TIME: 4–5 hours	
COST: $$$	

STAY: McCamly Plaza Hotel, Battle Creek, MI

PLAY: Gull Lake View Golf Course, Stonehenge Golf Course, Augusta, MI
Bedford Valley Golf Course, Battle Creek, MI

Ah, the McCamly Plaza Hotel. Has a certain style, a certain elegance to it, doesn't it? It is the preferred hotel in Battle Creek. During the week, business travelers are here; on weekends, it fills with golfers. It is a Triple-A, Four-Diamond hotel, the only such designee in Calhoun County, though we figure the standards must be a bit lower than in Cuyahoga County, because the place brags about having a Taco Bell and Pizza Hut on site. On the other hand, maybe the standards are higher; it is also home to Pablo's Jungle Restaurant. The hotel is connected to Kellogg Arena, the entertainment and trade-show Mecca for the area.

Fascinated as we were with Pablo's Jungle, we went to Porter's Steakhouse, on the top floor of the hotel, for our meals. We never looked back. In the morning, it sets out an all-American buffet: eggs and bacon, sausage, rolls, biscuits, coffee, and 'taters, and cereal. And best of all: fresh-squeezed orange juice.

It was Porter's for supper, too. Although the place is known for its beef, we also enjoyed the fish and pasta. Very generous portions here; no one leaves the table hungry. There is a children's menu available, and we found the service to be very good.

Porter's Cigar Bar has a walk-in humidor, good for maintaining cigars as well as keeping your cheeks wrinkle-free. It occurred to us that humidors such as this one provide aromatherapy. We know the New Agers will suggest we buzz off, but the rich smell of premium tobacco, like the rich smell of roasting coffee beans, is a delight whether you partake or not.

But here's the real reason we like it: the McCamly has a director of golf. True. It is Toby Hilton's job to make sure the golf part of the trip is pleasurable. He presents golf courses (nine of 'em!) like a three-card monty dealer presents cards—it looks so easy.

We note that while there is a director of golf, there is no director of kids, and though the area brags about the attractions for kids, we're not convinced they should be hauled along with the golf bags to Battle Creek. We loved a lot of what we found here—lodging, service, golf, and food, and those virtues will bring us back. But not with kids.

THE GOLF

We sampled three nearby golf courses.

At Gull Lake View, the first layout, West, was built in the early 1960s. A decade later, East was created. West has a wonderful, old-club feel to it as it rolls across hills and valleys. The back nine was recently updated with redesigned greens and sand bunkers. While East is shorter (we played from the back tees: 6,002 yards). It has more water and hills than West, so it's a target course. East is also a Certified Audubon Cooperative Sanctuary.

Just a short drive from there is Stonehedge, South and North. The South course is magnificent. If we could have played this track two or three times before leaving, we would have. Sculpted fairways, tall pines, and rock borders around the tee boxes make a beautiful course. It plays a little more than 6,600 yards from the back tees, a great challenge for single-digit handicaps. The forward tees here are 5,191, worth noting because it provides a challenge for red-tee players.

The North Course is open and easier. We loved it—six par 3s, six par 4s and six par 5s. Enough sand and water to inspire caution, but that's not the challenge. The challenge is understanding the wind.

Bedford Valley Golf Course is "the big course" here. One of the oldest in the area, it has been host to the Michigan Open, Michigan Senior Open, and the NCAA Division III National Championship. It's 6,800 yards to play where the champs play, with 47 traps, big greens, and often tough pin placements.

Battle Creek. Who would have thought that the home of Tony the Tiger could be so civilized?

ACCOMMODATIONS

McCamly Plaza Hotel   (616) 963-7050
50 Capital Ave. S.W., Battle Creek, MI

ROOMS: 242; **SUITES:** 6

ROOM RATES: $149–$169   **PAYMENT:** MC, VS, AX, DIS, DC

SPECIAL RATES: AAA (with card) $135 single/$145 double; AARP $135 single/$145 double; children under 18 free with parents

RESTAURANTS: Porter's Steakhouse (avg. entree $25), Porter's Cigar Bar

RESORT AMENITIES: indoor pool, health club, sauna, hot tub, cable TV/movies, room service, smoking rooms, non-smoking rooms, conference facilities

CONFERENCE/BUSINESS MEETING FACILITIES: executive conference center with 23 rooms for meetings, conferences, receptions, and seminars.

IF WE COULD HAVE PLAYED THIS TRACK TWO OR THREE TIMES BEFORE LEAVING, WE WOULD HAVE.

GOLF

GOLF PACKAGE RATES: $290 for 2 days and 3 rounds

PACKAGE INCLUDES: food/beverages, cart rental; weekend packages available

COURSES:

Gull Lake View Golf Course   (616) 731-4148
7147 N. 38th St., Augusta, MI

Stonehenge Golf Course   (616) 731-4148
15330 M-89, Augusta, MI

Bedford Valley Golf Course   (616) 965-3384
23161 Waubascon Rd., Battle Creek, MI

OTHER ATTRACTIONS NEARBY

Full Blast water park, Cereal City USA (cereal museum), Binder Park Zoo, John Harvey Kellogg Discovery Center, Leila Arboretum

DIRECTIONS

I-90 west; west on SR-2, north on I-280; south on I-75; west on I-475; north on US-23; north on I-69; west on I-94; exit 98B (downtown Battle Creek exit); left on Hamblin Ave.; 16 story building at next intersection.

YPSILANTI, MI
EAGLE CREST
RESORT

*Dress code: business casual
and golf togs.*

LOCATION: Southeast MI	
DRIVE TIME: 3–4 hours	
COST: $$	

STAY: The Marriott at Eagle Crest, Ypsilanti, MI

PLAY: Eagle Crest Golf Club, Ypsilanti, MI

NEARBY: University of Michigan

Eagle Crest Conference Resort in Ypsilanti has the conference center, of course, the Eagle Crest Golf Club, and a Marriott Hotel. The golf course and conference center are owned by Eastern Michigan University; the course is the home for its men's and women's golf teams. The course encircles the resort and conference center and plays for a number of holes along the banks of Ford Lake.

We think this stop is more business than pleasure. There is a honeymoon package, but unless the wedding is more merger than pledging of troths, this isn't the place. Let's face it: if your room has a data port, it is not for lovers.

The ballroom at the Marriott can comfortably handle more than 600 guests; the square footage dedicated to meetings, banquets, and exhibitions is more than 10,000. At the Eagle Crest conference center, spread out on 23,000 square feet are seven conference rooms, five seminar rooms, two auditoriums, an executive boardroom, and a computer lab. We never asked what the difference is between a seminar room and a conference room, satisfied that this place can do business.

LET'S FACE IT: IF YOUR ROOM HAS A DATA PORT, IT IS NOT FOR LOVERS

Marriott knows how to make us comfortable: king-sized bed, HBO on the tube, an office area, and a great view of the golf course. Sewing kit, ironing board and steam iron, coffee maker, and the usual batch of pleasant-smelling soaps and shampoos round out the room amenities. It is when we sit at the window, relaxing, enjoying coffee, and watching golfers, that we realize how challenging this game can be and what a high percentage of golfers have high handicaps.

Some of the pricing is oriented toward expense accounts. Charging

$8.95 for an in-room movie is steep, and 85 cents for directory assistance seems petty. Summarily adding a 17 percent tip to room service is insulting and adding a 55 percent surcharge to long distance calls is closer to stealing than to providing service.

While Marriott food and menu prices are somewhat predictable, so is the quality. Friendly wait staff here, and the breakfast buffet was everything a morning feast should be.

This is a convenient location for travelers with or without kids. Ypsi adjoins Ann Arbor, one of the great college towns in the U.S. There are a lot of waterways in this area for swimming and boating, and the park system encourages hiking. Detroit is just 30 miles away, so if vacation plans include music, the choices range from the Detroit Symphony to the Motown Museum. In nearby Dearborn is the Henry Ford Museum and Greenfield Village. Among the thousands of exhibits is the theater seat Abraham Lincoln was sitting in when John Wilkes Booth shot him.

THE GOLF

It's a handsome, playable course, and one of its greatest virtues is the lack of residential development. Club director Tom Pendlebury said, "You just don't see any housing developments. That's unusual for being this close to Detroit." You kidding? That's unusual for any new course.

Like many Michigan golf courses, Eagle Crest was once a dairy farm. Its original name, by the way, was the Huron Golf Club, but the university—in an effort to be politically correct?—changed it.

The green tees here are the longest and play 6,755 yards, par 72, course rating 73.6, and slope 138, which is obviously more golf course than most professionals can play at par or better. The blues are far more reasonable at 6,470 yards, which is a great challenge for good players playing the course for the first time. The slope on the blues is 135 and the course rating is 71.6. The whites measure 6,150 yards, par 72, slope 131, and course rating 70.7. The red tees here are a great length at 5,185 yards, and have a slope of 124 and a course rating of 69.7.

Nice little opening hole, from the whites, a 345-yard par 4. It bends a bit to the right, and a waterfall gurgles to the left of the green. The game is afoot at No. 2, a 395-yard par 4 that takes a dogleg left and has a green with water left and front. No. 6, the first par 5, has water all along the right side, and while the green is not difficult to hit in regulation, hitting it where it counts is a challenge: it's two-tiered.

On the back side, the tee box on No. 14 is gorgeous. This par 3 of 175 yards has a panoramic view of the course, the lake, and the surrounding area.

No. 16 is the hole for heroes. Over wetlands to a fairway that leans to the right, where Ford Lake waits. Water gets in the way of the approach; it's a peninsula green.

ACCOMMODATIONS

The Marriott at Eagle Crest   (734) 487-2000
1275 S Huron St., Ypsilanti, MI

ROOMS: 236; **SUITES:** 3

ROOM RATES: $85–$120   **PAYMENT:** checks, MC, VS, AX, DIS, DC

SPECIAL RATES: tee time package available

RESTAURANTS: Bentley's American Grill (avg. entree $7); Eagle Crest Grill (avg. entree $15)

RESORT AMENITIES: indoor pool, health club, sauna, hot tub, cable TV/movies, room service, smoking rooms, non-smoking rooms, conference facilities

CONFERENCE/BUSINESS MEETING FACILITIES: complete conference resort offering an IACC-approved conference center

GOLF

GOLF PACKAGE RATES: starting from $189/person for 1 day and 1 round

PACKAGE INCLUDES: breakfast, cart; weekend packages available

COURSE:

Eagle Crest Golf Club   (734) 487-2441
1275 S. Huron St., Ypsilanti, MI

OTHER ATTRACTIONS NEARBY

Henry Ford Museum, Wiards Orchard, Eastern Michigan University, University of Michigan, Briarwood Mall

DIRECTIONS

I-90 west; north on I-280; east on I-94; north on SR-23; east on SR-94; south on Huron St.; on left.

CHAUTAUQUA, NY
CHAUTAUQUA
INSTITUTION

Refreshing, rewarding,
awe-inspiring, and fun as hell

LOCATION: Southwest NY
DRIVE TIME: 2–3 hours
COST: $$$
....
STAY: The Spencer Hotel, Chautauqua, NY
PLAY: Chautauqua Golf Club, Chautauqua, NY

The Chautauqua Institution is a wonderful, even powerful, example of what can happen when education is taken from the hands of politicians, unionists, and bean counters, and placed squarely in the laps of educators. This gated community, which leans on the banks of Lake Chautauqua, celebrated its 125th anniversary a few years ago.

The season here is only nine weeks of summer. Jammed between opening and closing are arts and education programs, lectures, and entertainment that reflect the teaching philosophy of founders Lewis Miller and John Heyl Vincent, a brace of Methodists who in 1874 started the institution as the Chautauqua Lake Sunday School Assembly. It was an experimental, out-of-school vacation learning facility that was not only immediately successful, but immediately broadened its courses for Sunday school teachers to include music, art, and education.

Also jammed into the gated community during the season are 7,500 people residing here; 150,000 come for the scheduled public events. The small streets are lined with cottages, apartments, and hotels. The Chautauqua School of Fine and Performing Arts accepts more than 300 students each season and more than 400 open-enrollment special studies courses are offered.

The Institution covers a lakeside area about a mile long and a half-mile deep. It is crowded, but not painfully; it is busy, but never frantic. There is a shared intellectual purpose here, and it promotes camaraderie and a friendliness rarely seen. It is also dry.

In addition to the classrooms, concert halls, and galleries, the Institute has a square with administrative offices, some stores and restaurants, and a post office.

While it never preaches, the Institution was designed as a Christian facility, and that faith remains integral to the operation. We stopped at

Lutheran House, which provides housing for . . . yup, Lutherans on holiday. We also came across United Methodist House, the Episcopal House, and the Catholic House. The headquarters office for the United Church of Christ is here, too.

We stayed at the old and wonderful Spencer Hotel, a four-story frame only a couple hundred feet from the amphitheater, and our room, named the Jules Verne, featured a porch overlooking Palestine Street.

Helen Edgington is the proprietress of this Victorian delight, though steward might better describe her; the Spencer, after all, is in its third century. Carine Cherrualt is the manager, one of those rare women in the hospitality business who is exactly where she should be. She knows when the literary ghosts are dancing with guests and when the ghosts dance alone. She appreciates the serenity and beauty of the off season as well as the rushing madness of the season, when vacationers, nurturing their intellects, fill the streets, and walk quickly to lectures and concerts and classes. The Spencer is open all year.

Twenty-seven different rooms are available at the Spencer, all named for different authors. Ours featured a very firm king-sized bed decorated to look like a hot air balloon. The ceiling over the bed was painted to look in to the balloon above; the sheets resembled the wicker balloon basket, and around the sides of the bed were faux sandbags to loose when we set off on our 80-day tour around the world.

The Spencer sets a charming Continental breakfast table every morning. (Chocolate chip scones!) A more American breakfast was to be had at Sadie J's, on Institute grounds, where the owners' love for cats dominates every wall. No complaints with the bacon and eggs and toast on Styrofoam with plastic knife and fork. For dinner we went one night to Gianbrone's, just down the street from the Institute, and another night to the Italian Fisherman, in Bemus Point, across the bridge on the other side of Lake Chautauqua.

Worthy of note: the chicken Parmesan served at the Italian Fisherman is likely the best in the free world. A big place with dockside dining and broad windows that insist diners enjoy the view of the lake; make sure you have reservations.

And you make them, the hotel doesn't. Also, the Spencer doesn't have golf packages; you have to put the whole thing together yourself.

Is it worth it? Spending time at the Institution is refreshing, rewarding, awe-inspiring, and fun as hell.

THE GOLF

Off season at the Chautauqua Institution—now there's a golf get-away! The golf is secondary, but not second class. Just across the street from the Institution is the Chautauqua Golf Club. The club has 36 holes, the first 18 designed by the great Scotsman from Dornoch, Donald Ross and the second by golf architect Xen Hassenplug.

Stan Marshaus is the director of golf here, an East Cleveland native who graduated from Shaw High School in 1960 and Miami University (Ohio) five years later with a degree in mathematics.

He wanted to teach and coach, and he joined the faculty at Painesville Harvey High School as a basketball coach. It was then, at age 21, that he started playing golf.

His golf career took him in 1968 to the Arnold Palmer Golf Academy in Vail, Colorado. Over the next ten years, he would work for both Palmer and Jack Nickalus. But in 1978, when he accepted a position at Chautauqua GC, he found a home. He is more than director of golf here; he is an ardent cheerleader for the Institute. He has turned job offers away because he knows how blessed he is here. One of many benefits is playing golf with entertainers. Dinah Shore he found to be the efferves-cent charmer on the course as well as onstage. Johnny Mathis, Tony Bennett, and Willie Nelson have all enjoyed golf here. He has been very ac-tive with the PGA, even serving as announcer on the first tee at three PGA Championships.

Ross's course is the Lake Course, (6,148 yards, par 72 from the whites), and it is No. 7 that Marshaus likes. "It's a straightaway par 4, 420 yards through trees, but with no traps. Ben Hogan called it one of the greatest par 4s he had ever seen."

Hogan was one of many great professionals who conducted clinics at Chautauqua GC in the 1930s and '40s. Horton Smith, Sam Snead, and others were regulars there.

"Donald Ross was notorious for designing holes with lots of landing room," Marshaus said, "then a tough, tough approach to a very small green. He often had diffi-culty right and left, but none down the middle. He felt you should be able to roll it on, like they did in Scotland."

"BEN HOGAN CALLED IT ONE OF THE GREATEST PAR 4s HE HAD EVER SEEN"

No. 11 is another signature hole, "probably one of the great short par 4s," the director said. "It's only 360 yards, but it climbs a steep hill the last 100 yards." If you play short, you're in trouble.

The Hill Course looks like a member of the Ross family, and it plays 6,023 yards, par 72 from the whites. The course was built in 1985, and the dedication round was played with guests Clarence Rose and Mark Lye.

No. 4 offers risk and reward off the tee. It is a par 5 with a creek bisecting the fairway 227 yards out. Make it, and you've got a chance to get on in two. Miss it, and the ball sleeps with the fishes.

No. 13 is a par 3, only 165 yards, over water. If the flag is in front and the wind is swirling, club selection becomes, shall we say, challenging? And the best feature is the blooming, bright flower bed behind the green.

ACCOMMODATIONS

The Spencer Hotel   (800) 398-1306
25 Palestine Ave., Chautauqua, NY

ROOMS: 26; **SUITES:** 9

ROOM RATES: $165–$285   **PAYMENT:** checks

RESTAURANTS: The Spencer Hotel

RESORT AMENITIES: cable TV/movies, non-smoking rooms, conference facilities

CONFERENCE/BUSINESS MEETING FACILITIES: private suite for meetings

GOLF

GOLF PACKAGE RATES: call to put together package for variable number of days and variable number of rounds

PACKAGE INCLUDES: food/beverages, cart rental; weekend packages available; Sun–Thu packages available

COURSE:

Chautauqua Golf Club   (716) 357-6221
4731 W. Lake Rd., Chautauqua, NY

OTHER ATTRACTIONS NEARBY

NY wineries, Lucy & Desi Museum, historic walking tours, swimming, boating, water sports, art galleries, antiques shopping

DIRECTIONS

I-90 east to exit 60 for SR 394; south on SR-394; north on Elm Ln.; east on Hedding Ave.; south on Prospect Ave.; east on Palestine Ave.

ELLICOTTVILLE, NY HOLIDAY VALLEY RESORT

A getaway for outdoor family activities—and even the drive is fun

LOCATION: Southwest NY

DRIVE TIME: 3–4 hours

COST: $$$

....

STAY: The Inn at Holiday Valley, Ellicottville, NY

PLAY: Holiday Valley Resort Golf Course, Holiday Valley, NY

NEARBY: Allegheny State Park

We might as well tell you: we love Holiday Valley. We love Ellicottville, New York. We love buffalo steaks. The area has it all for a summer holiday: dramatic terrain, a sweet and wonderful history, plenty to do for kids and parents, a jazz festival, and a golf course that is truly sporty. Plus, the B & B Buffalo Ranch is nearby; we took steaks home and grilled them.

Even the ride was fun. Approaching western New York is a little like climbing the Rockies outside Denver (though smaller, of course): turn a corner and you're suddenly surrounded by pungent pines, bursts of yellow goldenrod, and rolling foothills.

The resort is at the edge of town, and Ellicottville is a friendly, laid-back town. It calls itself the Aspen of the East, wholly unnecessary. It has enough virtues to be Ellicottville. Just Ellicottville. The reference to Aspen is a reference to skiing. When the snow flies, the resort morphs, and skiers arrive to take over the hills. The town itself has quaint shops, historic red-brick buildings, and a beautifully renovated town hall that was nearly lost in a 1960 fire but saved from the wrecking ball and restored.

If it's like Aspen, it is Aspen without the pretense.

The charm of downtown reminded us of Ann Arbor in the summer, where walking and shopping and browsing and eating can all be done in a few delightful blocks.

At the Inn, we were impressed with the lobby. High ceilings, leather furniture, a massive stone fireplace, and a magnificent wood staircase. If Grizzly Adams had walked down the steps, we would have nonchalantly nodded in his direction. Our room had a back patio just 15 feet from a fairway. A brace of Adirondack chairs virtually insisted we sit and enjoy the moment.

No reason to lock the kids in the basement when you take this trip.

When you make reservations (and provide health histories) the kids can be dropped off at the fully-licensed day care center. Staying more than a day or two? There's the Mountain Adventure Kid's Camp, a day camp offering hiking, mountain biking, nature studies, and day trips of all sorts.

In addition to the buffalo ranch, there is the Griffis Sculpture Park, which has more than 200 huge metal sculptures created by local, national, and international artists. The stuff rests on 400 acres.

There are facilities here for meetings and conventions. A brand-new, state-of-the-art lodge has just been finished.

THE GOLF

The first nine, a traditional parkland design, was built in 1960. It remained a nine-hole track for more than 25 years, until the second nine was added, cutting across some of the lower ski slopes. The two nines are as different as Hoss and Little Joe. Walking the front nine is a pleasure; the back calls for help. The elevation changes, and narrow fairways carved through woods sometimes follow ski runs and are punctuated here and there by a sharp drop off, gorge, or ravine. Some holes course through winding gullies framed by steep banks. Only a mountain goat would feel comfortable walking here. And then only in daylight.

ONLY A MOUNTAIN GOAT WOULD FEEL COMFORTABLE WALKING HERE, AND THEN ONLY IN DAYLIGHT

One of the many treats here is the vistas from the tees. The majestic view goes for miles and miles and miles.

The course features bent grass greens and fairways, and a fully automated watering system. It is kept in immaculate condition.

Most of the tee boxes, built with railroad ties, are elevated and landscaped with flowers and ornamental grasses. So even if it's not a classic course, it's very pretty.

On the front nine, the "lower" nine, water comes into play on six holes. The ponds were here before the course and are used to feed the snow-making machines when it's time to ski. Speaking of time to ski, there are rare days in spring when it's possible to ski the upper slopes in the morning and play golf all afternoon.

There is a golf school here under the direction of head pro Dick Eaton.

No. 4 is the number one handicap hole, and standing at the tee, we said, "this is classic." A long par 4 with a slight dogleg left, it calls for length as well as accuracy. The green is heavily bunkered. Getting on in regulation makes it seem a bit of a pushover and hardly worth its number-one rating. But make an error at the tee or at the approach and the sleeping monster rolls over and bares its fangs.

No. 9 is another good one, this a short par 4 of 270 yards. Feelin' lucky? The green has a hidden pond at its left front and a big sand bunker on its right front.

On the back side, the fun begins by going uphill, up a ski run, actually; getting on in two means good judgment, two good shots, and an unshakable sense of balance. The need to maintain one's balance continues through the entire back side.

The fun starts on No. 11, another par 4. From this elevated tee, you're finally going to hit a drive just like the one the golf equipment salesman said you would with that new driver. Anybody can bomb it out there 250 yards, and big hitters go 350 yards. If the area looks familiar, this is parallel to No. 10, but instead of going up, it's going down. This 430-yard fun hole finishes uphill with a stonewalled creek and island green.

Getting to No. 13 is as much fun as playing it. While going up the cart path (and giving thanks for carts), it's not unusual to see some of the wildlife that lives here. This one is easier to play than describe. It's a par 5, but only 369 yards. It plays along a serpentine, super-narrow fairway with chasm to the left and high, steep bank to the right. Two hundred yards out, it bends very sharply left and begins its descent. Know what locals play to get on? Three 7-irons.

No. 15 is another downhill par 4, and this green is reachable for many players who didn't know they could drive a ball 313 yards.

That's what kind of course it is. It's a great deal of fun; it is often very challenging. It will make you want to play a second or third time.

ACCOMMODATIONS

The Inn at Holiday Valley   (716) 699-2345
SR 219, Ellicottville, NY

ROOMS: 95; **SUITES:** 7

ROOM RATES: $98–$209   **PAYMENT:** checks, MC, VS, AX, DIS

SPECIAL RATES: AAA, AARP

RESTAURANTS: Hearth Restaurant (avg. entree $11), McCarty Cafe

RESORT AMENITIES: indoor pool, outdoor pool, health club, sauna, hot tub, cable TV/movies, smoking rooms, non-smoking rooms, conference facilities

CONFERENCE/BUSINESS MEETING FACILITIES: meeting space available for up to 500; rooms range from private board rooms to banquet facilities; food and beverage service can be tailored to your needs; group or team-building activities can be arranged.

SPECIAL PROGRAMS FOR CHILDREN: summer day camp for ages 5–11: activities include hiking, fishing, golf, swimming, group games, nature studies, crafts, and a camp-out one night a week.

GOLF

GOLF PACKAGE RATES: early season (before May 17): $278/weekday (2 people), $337/weekend (2 people); Summer (5/18–10/24): $335/weekday (2 people), $419/weekend (2 people) for 2 days and 2 rounds

PACKAGE INCLUDES: Continental breakfast, cart rental, unlimited range balls, club cleaning & storage; weekend packages available; Sun–Thu packages available; custom packages available for families, couples, and serious players

COURSE:

Holiday Valley Resort Golf Course   (716) 697-2345
SR 219, Holiday Valley, NY

OTHER ATTRACTIONS NEARBY

Village of Ellicottville (restaurants, bars, shopping, galleries, entertainment), Allegheny State Park, Griffis Sculpture Park, Salamanca Rail Museum, Seneca Nation Museum, Amish farms and shops

DIRECTIONS

I-90 east to exit 10A for SR-86; east on SR-86 to exit 21 for Salamanc); north on SR-219 to Holiday Valley.

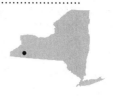

FINDLEY LAKE, NY
PEEK 'N PEAK RESORT

All the charm of a quaint, comfortable New England town

LOCATION: Southwest NY

DRIVE TIME: 2–3 hours

COST: $$$

....

STAY: Peek 'n Peak Resort & Conference Center, Findley Lake, NY

PLAY: Peek 'N Peak Lower Course and Upper Course, Findley Lake, NY

NEARBY: Chautauqua Institution

How can you not like a resort that lifts a line from Aristotle for its brochure? "In all things of nature is something of the marvelous," the ancient Greek said.

This place is more than a resort, it's a village—with a challenging miniature golf course (with real flagsticks), bicycle rentals, a golf school, a public driving range, condominiums, rental suites, homes, a gas station, two golf courses, and the Inn at the Peak Lodge.

The Inn is an impressive white-and-dark-chocolate-brown gem. It looks as if it were plucked out of the Alps. Restaurants include the Garden Coffee Shop (we're suckers for Texas toast) with some outdoor seating and the Royal Court Dining Room.

The grandeur of the Royal is highlighted by a magnificent stone fireplace. A quarry must have been emptied for all the stone used to build it. Seafood and steaks are the specialties, and the entrees begin with a house salad that has grapefruit and strawberries. For those who enjoy the added delight, the wine cellar here is an accomplished one.

Dessert, we regret to report, is a chocolate chip walnut pie, served warm and so good we seriously considered having it after breakfast and lunch.

Our digs were comfortable and had all the amenities we've grown accustomed to: hair dryer, coffee maker, and iron and ironing board. The Golf Channel is on the telly, and a fresh newspaper appears at the door every morning.

There are two swimming pools here—the one indoors is open late, and the one outdoors is open 'til dusk. On one end is a pool for kids, and yes, we were the guests who gave in to temptation and were running back and forth through the fountains and gliding down the waterslide. The hot tub is an inside-outside affair. If it's too warm indoors, swim the channel to the outside portion. The workout facility puts many gyms to shame, and there are also a tanning booth, sauna, game room, indoor and outdoor tennis courts, a playground, and patio areas that we found delightful.

PULLING IN TO THE TOWN OF FINDLEY LAKE, WE HALF EXPECTED BOB NEWHART TO WELCOME US

All this after a brief two-hour drive? Pulling in to the town of Findley Lake, we half-expected Bob Newhart to welcome us. With quaint shops, a water wheel, fishermen on a mist-covered lake, and a garden where you pick your own bouquet, it looks like his Vermont television town.

The place is known as a ski resort, but with two good courses and the Inn, there are plenty of good reasons to come here year round.

THE GOLF

Golf started here in the early 1970s when the Lower Course was built. They were thinking of us when they designed this layout. It begins with a par 5, which we think is the way all courses should start play. At a some-what short 475 yards, the gentle dogleg left is a great introduction to the course. We often look back when we play because we find great views, and that's what happened on No. 1 here. We looked back to see the Lodge nestled in Mother Nature's arms.

There are only two sets of tees on this course. The men's tees play 6,260 yards, the women's lay 5,328 yards. We found it to be one of the best courses for mixed-couple matches. Slope is 115, and course rating is 69.0. While it's a playable course, there are some surprises here for the unwary.

No. 5 is the other long one on the front side. At 530 yards, it's a three-shotter for most of us. The creek that slides across the fairway gives play-ers pause. A creek meanders throughout, and a lake on No. 6 means car-rying fishermen. At 178 yards, the par 3 No. 8 is a tester.

No. 9 wins our vote for the most handsome hole. A 375-yard par 4, the Inn and the mountains form the backdrop. The approach over water finds a bridge filled with flower boxes.

The back nine has fewer traps and virtually no water, so it's gorgeous play. Until No. 17. This 509-yard par 5 is an S-shaped challenge, and the green is tucked behind a grove of trees. It's the second shot here that's most important; coming up short on it means a virtual bogey.

The golf school here is Roland Stafford, a veteran teaching facility. Nice to have a highly-regarded school as part of the resort. We've found that taking even a brief lesson when we arrive tends to settle our nerves, focus our games, and help us play better. Might be all psychological, but still.

There are beverage carts circling the courses—always a nice touch. Both courses, by the way, have restaurants and decks overlooking the home holes. We enjoyed double-decker turkey sandwiches between rounds.

Thus fortified, we took on the Upper Course. Might as well 'fess up— it took us 10 more on the Upper than we needed on the Lower.

The Lower Course is somewhat flat, even easily walkable. It is short. For all its physical beauty, ambushes are easy to see and play around.

The Upper Course, added 20 years after the Lower Course opened, is pack-mule steep. It has four sets of tees (6,888 yards to 4,835 yards), ten forced carries (beginning with two over ravines on the first hole), and a par 3 with such a steep drop that our 120-yard club worked perfectly on this 172-yard hold. And let us quickly add that the par 3s, front and back on the Upper Course, are worth the price of admission.

We played the blue tees, which measure 3,111 yards going out and 3,316 coming in, and it was more course than we were players. But, we said over cocktails later, we were virgins sacrificed at the Altar of Bogey. Next time we play, we'll know a lot more.

If we weren't cowardly, we would have tried to drive No. 3, a 317-yard par 4 that looks, from the tee at least, drivable. We told ourselves the air is thinner. We had just finished a high-protein turkey sandwich, and driving the green would mean eternal bragging rights. Did we mention the hole was downhill? Too bad the bunker in front of the green is so big that a car, we were told, was once buried there. We choked.

No. 9 is the number one handicap, a long and beautiful par 5 of 502 yards. There is both water and sand on this hole that bends almost imperceptibly left as it continues.

The back nine emerges from the woods and plays on a more open

field. The number two handicap is also a par 5. No. 14 stretches 550 yards, and the trapping on this hole, both fairway and green, is particularly good.

ACCOMMODATIONS

Peek 'n Peak Resort & Conference Center   (716) 355-4141
1405 Olde Rd., Findley Lake, NY

ROOMS: 108; **SUITES:** 36

ROOM RATES: $131–$350   **PAYMENT:** checks, MC, VS, AX, DIS, DC

SPECIAL RATES: AAA, AARP, corporate (weekday), kids under 18 stay free

RESTAURANTS: Royal Court Dining Room (avg. entree $25), Tavern on the Tee, Woods & Wedges

RESORT AMENITIES: indoor pool, outdoor pool, health club, sauna, hot tub, cable TV/movies, room service, smoking rooms, non-smoking rooms, babysitting service, conference facilities, golf school, miniature golf, water slide, cabana bar, lawn games, complimentary bikes

CONFERENCE/BUSINESS MEETING FACILITIES: nine banquet and conference rooms and three lodges accommodate groups from 2 to 600; the Team Dynamics Team Building Programs includes a 24-element ropes course

SPECIAL PROGRAMS FOR CHILDREN: Peek 'n Peak Kids Summer Club features supervised activities for children ages 6–11

GOLF

GOLF PACKAGE RATES: $128–$322/person, double occupancy ($124/person weekdays) for 1–2 days and 1 round

PACKAGE INCLUDES: cart rental; weekend packages available; Sun–Thu packages available

COURSE:

Peek 'N Peak Lower Course and Upper Course   (716) 355-4141
1405 Olde Rd., Findley Lake, NY

OTHER ATTRACTIONS NEARBY

Chautauqua Institution, Lake Chautauqua, Double DAB Riding Stables, Presque Island State Park, NY & PA wineries, Niagara Falls, Roger Tory Peterson Institute of Natural History, Findley Lake Shops, antiques shopping

DIRECTIONS

I-90 east to exit 37 for I-86; I-86 to exit 4 for Findley Lake; right on SR-426; south to Peek 'n Peak; on right.

135

BEAVER FALLS, PA
BLACK HAWK

Close-by, comfortable, uncomplicated

LOCATION: Western PA
DRIVE TIME: 1–2 hours
COST: $$
....

STAY: Holiday Inn, Beaver Falls, PA
PLAY: Rolling Acres Golf Course, Beaver Falls, PA

B eaver Falls is one of those places that is so close you can make reservations over the phone and get there before your room is ready. You only need to go to the second exit on the Pennsylvania Turnpike.

The Holiday Inn there had everything we needed and more: indoor pool, sauna and whirlpool, game room, guest laundry, and Casey's Grill. We made good use of the ironing board in our room. Golf is more than a game, of course; it is often a fashion show, and showing up in a wrinkled Cutter & Buck shirt and Armani slacks without a crisp crease is a misdemeanor in some states. We knew we were in trouble when Johnston & Murphy started making golf shoes. So being able to touch up the wardrobe before stepping onto the first tee is handy.

The hotel has an indoor pool with three- to nine-foot depths. There is no children's area, so it's best suited to kids who know how to swim. The pool area also has men's and women's saunas and a whirlpool. It is set up like a tropical courtyard, and the rooms that face the courtyard have a patio area that overlooks the pool. There are a lot of poolside chairs, and next to the pool area is an indoor playset for children. Our four-year-old did his best imitation of a chimpanzee on the swings, slides, monkey bars, and play fort. Also in this area is a ping-pong table, pool table, and foosball game—all free. Video games are here, and the exercise room has treadmills and exercise bikes.

The bar and grill has a baseball motif, and it was carried out well. There are two huge leather chairs built to look like baseball mitts (a staff person said each chair cost five grand). The booth we sat in was like a dugout. We enjoyed it, and The Heir loved it.

We tossed our own sage advice out the window when we ordered. Here we were, on the western edge of Pennsylvania, and we ordered crab cakes and Caesar salad with salmon. The four-year-old plowed through a plate of chicken fingers, though we learned last year not to call the dish chicken fingers, but only chicken.

THE GOLF

Many courses have names that don't reflect the course at all. Rolling Acres however, is accurately descriptive of this course's wonderful terrain. This rolling course is also spotted with a half dozen lakes, and every one of them comes into play. The first 18 holes were built in 1965. In the 1990s, a third nine was added.

The fairways feature bent grass and are watered; the large greens have a combination of bent and poa anna. While it could be said the course is lightly bunkered, half of the bunkers are grass.

There are three tee positions, and the North and South configuration (the original 18) can be stretched out to 6,580 yards. The West course is a playable 2,864 yards.

Two holes stand out here: No. 9 and No. 18 on the North–South track. The former is only 351 yards, but the hole comes into the clubhouse and rises as it nears the sand-protected green. It's pleasant later to watch other players come in for the turn from the big deck that rises above the green. And the home hole is a hole for heroes: 436 yards, and it's uphill. It takes a big drive to get started on this one and an even better shot to get on: the green is small, and holding it is like holding a cat and trimming its nails. Too much stick means rolling over the green into the woods, or, as head pro Bob Lambert, PGA, says, "That's jail."

Nice as the course is, the new clubhouse is what makes eyebrows rise. It's called The Timberhouse, and with good reason. Twelve-by-twelve timbers make up the frame, and the decor reminded us of a ski lodge. It's big enough to handle a wedding reception downstairs in the hall while the Bachelors Club meets upstairs.

ACCOMMODATIONS

Holiday Inn   (724) 846-3700
7195 Eastwood Rd., Beaver Falls, PA

ROOMS: 156

ROOM RATES: $85–$120   **PAYMENT:** checks, MC, VS, AX, DIS

RESTAURANTS: Casey's (avg. entree $13)

RESORT AMENITIES: indoor pool, health club, sauna, hot tub, cable TV/movies, room service, pets welcome, smoking rooms, non-smoking rooms, conference facilities

CONFERENCE/BUSINESS MEETING FACILITIES: can accommodate meetings and seminars

GOLF

GOLF PACKAGE RATES: $89–$169 for 1–2 days and 1–3 rounds

PACKAGE INCLUDES: cart rental

COURSE:

Rolling Acres Golf Course (724) 843-6736
350 Anchortown Rd., Beaver Falls, PA

OTHER ATTRACTIONS NEARBY

shopping, restaurants

DIRECTIONS

I-80 east to I-76; right on New Castle Interchange; exit 1a for New
Castle/Pittsburgh; north on SR-60 to New Castle; north on SR-351 to
New Galillee/Koppell; left on Shenango Rd.; right on Fairlane Blvd.;
right on Eastwood Rd.

THIS ROLLING
COURSE IS
SPOTTED WITH A
HALF DOZEN
LAKES, AND EVERY
ONE OF THEM
COMES INTO PLAY.

BLAIRSVILLE, PA
CHESTNUT RIDGE
& TOM'S RUN

*Particularly good
for the not-so-fair sex*

LOCATION: Western PA
DRIVE TIME: 3–4 hours
COST: $$

STAY: Chestnut Ridge Inn on the Green, Blairsville, PA
PLAY: Chestnut Ridge Golf Club & Tom's Run Golf Course, Blairsville, PA
NEARBY: Idlewild Amusement Park

Some golf packages are better suited for men, the regular foursomes that play together and travel together. The requirements are these: the place has to have great golf, and we have to be able to play 36 a day; the food has to be very good; the television has to get ESPN. Other than that, we don't really care if there's a discount mall, a beach, a Cineplex, or a historical marker.

The Chestnut Ridge Inn on the Green Resort satisfies these needs. Two award-winning courses, two excellent restaurants (one good diner, too), and spartan but comfortable shelter provided just down the street at the Comfort Inn. It is not luxurious. It is spotless. A very good Continental breakfast is assembled every morning and offered without charge to guests. It has a very friendly staff.

TWO AWARD-WINNING COURSES, TWO EXCELLENT RESTAURANTS, AND SPARTAN BUT COMFORTABLE SHELTER The men's locker room here is better than in most private clubs, and the pro shop is stocked with very nice stuff.

If forced at gunpoint, you can take the kids, but remember: they have to be fascinated with four covered bridges in the area and shocked and delighted to learn Jimmy Stewart was born around here. And they have to enjoy listening to you drone on and on about, *It's A Wonderful Life*. Trust us, this part of life is wonderful sans wives and kids.

The resort is a memorial to Martin Bearer, a local businessman and entrepreneur. His formal education ended in seventh grade; his business education began with a home delivery route for coal. He derived his pleasures from work, yet laughed often and told stories well. He didn't golf. He collected art and statuary, much of it now part of the resort and the courses today. He bought the resort in the late 1970s and added Tom's Run golf course as well as the new half of the resort facility. A couple years ago, pancreatic cancer killed him.

Chestnut Ridge—the ridge itself—is on the horizon. It is part of the Laurel Highlands, and while we first think of Rolling Rock longnecks when we hear that, this area also serves up one of the Keystone State's other bottled treats: Hank's Premium Philadelphia Vanilla Cream Soda. It comes in brown longnecks. One of many delights for the senses on this trip.

The pro shop is home to the two restaurants here, the Crystal Terrace, where service is exquisite (the ceiling features a huge and glorious stained glass window salvaged from a local church that met the wrecker's ball), and Le Fleur. We ate only at the Terrace and assume the food and service at Le Fleur, which is more casual, is equally good.

Among the appetizers at the Terrace are capelli pasta and crab Hoelzel. The pasta is tossed with fresh tomatoes, peppers, black olives, basil, garlic, and a little Parmesan cheese. The crab is lump crab meat with a light tarragon and black pepper vinaigrette. We loved the mushroom soup that was flavored with sherry and fresh cream. There are a few worthwhile salads, especially the fresh spinach, and the entrees are a carnivore's dream: lamb chops, filet mignon, delmonico steak, pork tenderloin, and noisettes of veal. (Don't ask us. We thought a noisette was the sound a little kid makes as you teach him to blow his nose.) From the seas come scallops, lobster tails, Maryland crab cakes, rainbow trout, salmon, and yellow fin tuna. The tablecloths are nicely starched and the service is professional.

Few golf packages offer food and dining service on a par with this place.

THE GOLF

There are two golf courses here: Chestnut Ridge, which was built in 1963, and Tom's Run (named for a creek than runs through it), which was built in 1993.

Each is distinctive. Both courses have been honored by being in *Golf Digest*'s "Places to Play," and Tom's Run is rated "No. 6 Best Public Golf Course in Pennsylvania."

Head golf professional Dave Kuhar loves asking guests, "Which did you like more?" After playing both courses, we could only answer, "Could we play a few more times before deciding?" Lots of drama on

both courses, plenty of physical beauty and a great golf challenge.

At Chestnut Ridge, the whites play 6,027, par 72, slope 125; from the blues, it's 6,321, par 72, slope 129. The older course surprised us with drama at the tee boxes, especially No. 6, which backs in to the clubhouse, and from its elevated position provides a magnificent view of the hole, adjacent holes, the valley, and the ridge in the distance. The back side has three par 5s, three par 4s, and three par 3s. The view leaving the green at No. 10 is awesome, and the view from the tee box at No. 11 maintains the natural wonder. The course is challenging, beautiful, playable, and well cared for. It reminds of us a poli-sci prof we had in college.

Tom's Run is different but equally challenging and beautiful. From the whites, it's 6,266, par 72, slope of 129. While it is not a long track, players are cautioned to use the white tees unless they play to a single digit. The blues stretch matters out to 6,812, par 72, but the slope is 134.

The opening hole can be deceiving—it plays a little longer than it looks and at 407 yards, two good shots are called for to get on in regulation. It has a generous, open landing area, and sand guards the green.

Nos. 2, 3, and 4 are the three most exciting consecutive holes we've found in golf—a par 3 (140 yards), a par 4 (314 yards), and a par 5 (442 yards.) The par 3 is from a cliff into the valley, and the next two play in the valley before climbing out. On No. 2, proper club selection and a keen understanding of Kentucky windage are called for. On Nos. 3 and 4, golf smarts are required. For this wonderful trio, where length is hardly necessary, only shotmakers will emerge with par or better.

OTHER STATES : PENNSYLVANIA

Climbing up the steep hill to leave the valley, we came across a wonderful sculpture of a cowboy thrown by his bucking horse. It's exemplifies the artwork that is such a part of this course.

Chestnut Ridge is the sort of resort traditions are built upon.

ACCOMMODATIONS

Chestnut Ridge Inn on the Green   (800) 770-0000
1762 Old William Penn Hwy., Blairsville, PA

ROOMS: 70; **SUITES:** 8

ROOM RATES: $89–$119   **PAYMENT:** MC, VS, AX, DIS, DC

SPECIAL RATES: children under 18, groups, seniors, AAA, AARP

RESORT AMENITIES: indoor pool, health club, cable TV/movies, smoking rooms, non-smoking rooms, conference facilities

CONFERENCE/BUSINESS MEETING FACILITIES: can accommodate meetings and seminars

GOLF

GOLF PACKAGE RATES: $69–$139 for 1 day and 1 round

PACKAGE INCLUDES: food/beverages, cart rental; weekend packages available;
Sun–Thu packages available

COURSE:

Chestnut Ridge Golf Club & Tom's Run Golf Course   (724) 459-7188
1762 Old William Penn Hwy., Blairsville, PA

OTHER ATTRACTIONS NEARBY

Idlewild Amusement Park, Jimmy Stewart Museum, antiques shopping

DIRECTIONS

I-80 east; south on I-79 to exit 99 for Butler/New Castle; east on US-422 to Butler; take US-119; left on William Penn Hwy.

THE MEN'S LOCKER ROOM IS BETTER THAN MOST PRIVATE CLUBS.

BOLIVAR, PA
CHAMPION LAKES

*Pittsburgh Pirates fans
will be delighted*

LOCATION: Western PA
DRIVE TIME: 3–4 hours
COST: $

....

STAY: Champion Lakes Golf Club / Bed & Breakfast, Bolivar, PA
PLAY: Champion Lakes Golf Club, Bolivar, PA
NEARBY: Idlewild Amusement Park

When today's ballplayers retire, money will be the least of their concerns. Food on the table and shoes on the kids will cause no worry. But just a generation ago, retiring athletes had to go to work.

Jerry Lynch and Dick Groat, teammates on the Pittsburgh Pirates and veterans of three World Series, still had to make ends meet when they hung it up in the early 1960s.

They designed and built Champion Lakes Golf Club, just outside historic Ligonier, Pennsylvania, an hour east of Pittsburgh and three hours from Cleveland. The bed and breakfast opened in 1995.

It took the ballplayers two years before they found the right piece of land, and more than three decades later, they still own it. Dick is active in the day-to-day operation. Jerry frequently visits from Atlanta. Both were there the day we played, and we enjoyed dinner together. They skipped dessert to watch the first game of the World Series.

Over the years, all of their kids worked at the course, and today Allison Groat-DeStefano is the director of golf. When she gets the chance, she can play in the mid-70s. Working around the course as a kid provided her a golf scholarship to James Madison University.

The B & B is a nine-room, sports-themed cottage including a Players Lounge, which can be used as a king-sized suite if you like. The B & B can accommodate up to 18, and the rooms are named after Pirates players from the early '60s. Pictures of the players, fresh-faced and in their playing primes, reminded us how fast time flies. Each room has private bath, air conditioning, and color TV with HBO.

The package includes breakfast and lunch. It's standard fare and pretty good. If you have a large group, dinner can be had at the B & B,

but for most guests, dinner is where you find it—we found it in Ligonier.

For non-golfers, Ligonier (and Fort Ligonier) are delightful. There are lots of shops, some very nice antique stores, and great restaurants. The Idlewild Amusement Park is close by and so is Latrobe, Pennsylvania, famous for Arnold Palmer and Rolling Rock beer. Plus this is just a pretty part of the country.

THE GOLF

How a pair of baseball players managed to put together a course this good will remain one of life's great mysteries, but they did, and it has stood the test of time.

It plays 6,608 from the blues, 6,205 from the whites, 5,558 from the reds. Arrogant players, strutting around the back of the box to play the blues, are humbled here. For a long time, the King held the course record—and we're not talking Elvis. The real King, Arnold Palmer, fired a 68 from the tips one day. He plays out of nearby Laurel Valley Golf Club. His score was bettered by PGA Tour pro Rocco Mediate, who holds the current course record of 65.

The course looks good on this terrain, the result of thoughtful routing and very good design. We found elevated tees, elevated greens, sloping fairways, sidehill, uphill, and downhill lies, big greens (in wonderful condition). The views alone are worth the price of the greens fees; during fall, words cannot adequately describe the natural beauty.

The holes include wide, hazard-free fairways and tree-lined fairway alleys where any shot off line costs. (This is especially true on the doglegs.)

The number two handicap is No. 13, its signature hole. It plays 407 yards and insists on a blind tee shot that has to carry water (150 from the whites, 188 from the blues) and stay in the short grass. As the hole rises and bends right, mature hardwoods line both sides. Once settled on the left or center/left side of the fairway, the green becomes accessible. But a nice drive that holds on the right side of this sloping right-to-left fairway doesn't help much; trees block the approach.

This is a good example of the course; it calls for shotmaking skills yet is not unfair.

While it may not look it, Champion Lakes is a great course to walk and carry. And having an owner on site means the little things are taken care of—carts clean and gassed, scorecards, sharp pencils, and clean bathrooms.

Much of the play comes from Pittsburgh and the Allegheny County area, but groups from Columbus and Cincinnati make annual pilgrimages. A few years ago, a larger-than-expected number of players from Columbus arrived. Allison set up cots for them in the bar area. They loved it.

ACCOMMODATIONS

Champion Lakes Golf Club/Bed & Breakfast   (724) 238-5440
Rd #1 Box 285, Bolivar, PA

ROOMS: 9; **SUITES:** 1

ROOM RATES: $65–$85   **PAYMENT:** checks, MC, VS, AX

SPECIAL RATES: AAA: $65/person

RESTAURANTS: Champion Lakes Bed & Breakfast

RESORT AMENITIES: cable TV/movies, 4 bedroom home on 16th tee available

CONFERENCE/BUSINESS MEETING FACILITIES: banquet facilities accommodating up to 150

GOLF

GOLF PACKAGE RATES: $65–$184 for 1–3 days and unlimited rounds

PACKAGE INCLUDES: breakfast, cart rental

COURSE:

Champion Lakes Golf Club   (724) 238-5440
285 Rd. 1, Bolivar, P

OTHER ATTRACTIONS NEARBY

Idlewild Amusement Park; Historic Ligonier (Fort Ligonier, Compass Inn Museum, antiques); Johnstown Flood Museum

DIRECTIONS

I-80 east; east on PA Turnpike to exit 9 for Donegal; north on SR-711; on left.

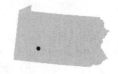

CHAMPION, PA
SEVEN SPRINGS
MOUNTAIN RESORT

A gorgeous getaway to
Pennsylvania's Laurel Highlands

LOCATION: Southwest PA
DRIVE TIME: 3–4 hours
COST: $$$

STAY: Seven Springs Mountain Resort, Champion, PA
PLAY: Seven Springs Mountain Resort Golf Course, Champion, PA
NEARBY: Idlewild Amusement Park

Here's our first suggestion, and we don't care if we sound like nerds: take the scenic history tour. It's a shuttle bus through the resort and the surrounding Laurel Highlands, and it's worthwhile. You'll learn not only about the history of this resort originally built for skiers but also about the dreams of the founders, Helen and Adolph Dupre. The tour is free. (As long as we're on our nerd bandwagon, this place is polka heaven, with four polka events between spring and fall; if you're at a polka and not having fun, you must be dead.)

In 1932, the founders plunked down their entire savings, $13, to buy two and a half acres. The area reminded them of their native Bavaria. Over the next couple of decades, they built their own house and 28 cabins, all from native wood and stone. Three years after starting, Dupre built a mechanical tow rope powered by a Packard engine. In 1937, the place was open and thriving with slopes named Suicide Hill, Hell's Highway, and Nosedive. A year later, the private Seven Springs Club was founded with 50 members. Along the way, summer activities were becoming more important, and more and more land was added. By 1948, it stretched to 10,000 acres. The place grew faster than the budget in the hands of a Democratic Congress.

The marketing department trumpets, "The fun doesn't end when the snow melts." Perhaps, but we'd say, "Maybe after golf season there are other things to do here." There's a lot to do here *during* golf season: a wine fest in August, the Labor Day Jazz Festival, the Mid-Year's Eve

party—these mountain folk clearly like to party.

The wine fest is more impressive than you might think: more than a dozen area vintners join forces with musicians, artisans, and chefs to put on a weekend to remember. There are wine seminars where you will learn how nonsensical it is to smell a cork (unless you drink your wine from a cork vessel, of course). And yes, there's a grape-stomping contest, but we don't want to know what is done with the juice.

Five thousand guests can sleep in the ten-story high-rise, chalets, condos, and cabins. In addition to the great golf course, there is roller skating, racquetball, bowling, and tennis. There is also a good kids' program here and hayrides every night.

A lot of businesses know about Seven Springs: every year, about 700 conferences are held here. How you can keep your mind on business with the Laurel Highlands out back is beyond us, though. The dining options we enjoyed were Helen's, an elegant restaurant named after the founder, and the Oak Room, which is on the fourth floor of the main lodge. Helen's is a little more sophisticated, and reservations are often made far in advance. The Oak Room is a bit on the casual side, and reservations are unnecessary. The dinner and breakfast buffets, and the seafood on Friday, were excellent.

THE GOLF

Now here's a designer we haven't heard of before: German native Xem Hasenplug. The course he designed is magnificent, taking great advantage of the terrain, but never overstepping the bounds of good design. No trick holes, nothing unfair.

The great physical beauty of the course begins at the first tee and is duplicated on No. 10. There is very little water on this course, and the bunkering is judicious. Hasenplug must have enjoyed laying this out. He slips in sloped greens and canted fairways on the 6,166-yard layout.

The number one handicap is No. 5, a 517-yard par 5 that begins with an uphill drive, adds a severe dogleg left, offers sand on the right as the green gets close, and presents a small green. Oh, and it's O.B. the whole right side.

No. 9, a 328-yard par 4, is another uphill hole with the parking lot on the right. There is a free drop at point of entry, then it's off to the back side and the magnificent view No. 10 offers. They call Nos. 11 and 12 their "Amen Corner." The former is a 197-yard par 3, a downhill hole with both water and sand at the green. The latter calls for a straight drive of 220 yards to reach the top of the hill. From there, it's all downhill on this 393-yard par 4.

The most challenging hole on the course is the number-two-handicap No. 17, a 425-yard par 4, with O.B. right and a well-protected green. No. 18 is no pushover: 374 yards and it calls for a drive to get "over the hump." The green is two-tiered.

ACCOMMODATIONS

Seven Springs Mountain Resort   (800) 452-2223
777 Waterwheel Dr., Champion, PA

ROOMS: 385; **SUITES:** 12

ROOM RATES: $165–$720   **PAYMENT:** checks, MC, VS, DIS

RESTAURANTS: Oak Room (avg. entree $25), Helen's, Coffee Shop, Slopeside Grill

RESORT AMENITIES: indoor pool, outdoor pool, hot tub, cable TV/movies, babysitting service, conference facilities

CONFERENCE/BUSINESS MEETING FACILITIES: extensive convention facilities to accommodate meetings of any size

SPECIAL PROGRAMS FOR CHILDREN: kids' Adventure Kamp, a full- or half-day camp for children from walking age to 12 years old, features fishing, treasure hunts, arts and crafts, slip-n-slide, and swimming.

GOLF

GOLF PACKAGE RATES: $135–$230 for 1–3 days and unlimited rounds

PACKAGE INCLUDES: cart rental

COURSE:

Seven Springs Mountain Resort Golf Course   (800) 452-2223
777 Waterwheel Dr., Champion, PA

OTHER ATTRACTIONS NEARBY

Fallingwater, Idlewild Amusement Park, Fort Ligonier

DIRECTIONS

I-80 east; east on to PA Turnpike to exit 9 for Donegal; east on SR-31; south on SR-711; left on County Line Rd.; 8 miles ahead on right.

EDINBORO, PA
CULBERTSON HILLS
& RIVERSIDE

No frills, but the golf thrills

LOCATION: Northwest PA
DRIVE TIME: 2–3 hours
COST: $
....
STAY: Edinboro Inn, Edinboro, PA
PLAY: Culbertson Hills Golf Resort,
Edinboro, PA
Riverside Golf Club, Cambridge
Springs, PA

When Don Franceski and I saw Edinboro on the list of getaways, we couldn't wait to go. Not only is Edinboro a pretty college town just a little ways across the Pennsylvania state line, and not only does it have two great and different courses, and not only are the prices more than reasonable, but we've been there before.

Years ago, Don used to lead a couple dozen guys to Edinboro for a few days of golf and a few nights of drinking and poker. Truth to tell, back then we didn't find much for the family, but then again, we weren't looking for it.

We checked in at the Edinboro Inn—the same place we stayed years ago. The college campus, of course, is pretty, and the swimming pool at the hotel was doing a great trade in screaming kids, but all we were headed straight to the first tee. The hotel is, how should we put this ... well, it's a bit on the spartan side. But clean, simple rooms were all we needed on this trip.

And right next door is one of the most interesting courses in the area, Culbertson Hills Golf Resort. In addition to an historic course, there's a small bar where lunch is served.

THE GOLF

The course is owned and maintained by the Orr Brothers: Gary, Robert (PGA) and Donald. The course has grass bunkers and no sand. It also boasts towering hardwoods and wonderful greens. It was designed by Thomas Bendelow—not a name often brought up by golfers, but that's an omission. Bendelow, a Scotsman, also designed Butler CC and Medinah No. 3. Culbertson's blood lines are impressive.

We liked this course so much that after we totaled our scores and paid the bets, we went back to the first tee and played it again. The course rolls

gently and has a few memorable holes. No. 3
comes to mind almost immediately. A long
par 3 of 200 yards to an elevated green, it
looks far more difficult than it plays. Some
regulars think No. 7 is the signature here, a
very challenging 361-yard par 4 that bends a
bit to the right setting up an approach over water. And No. 9, a par 5 of
570 yards, is a three-shot hole for most of us. The ninth green doesn't
bring players back to the clubhouse, so play, in our opinion, is faster.
Having some groups stop for a sandwich or a cold drink is a waste of
valuable golf time. From the whites, it plays 6,395 yards, a long course for
some middle- and high-handicappers. The blue tees are 6,813, a long
ways in 1931, when the course was founded.

If the only course we played was Culbertson Hills, we wouldn't have
any complaints, but we toured Riverside Golf Club, too, and found a
wonderful, lush, 18-hole course with all the amenities: pro shop, locker
rooms, full service restaurant, and bar.

For two days in a row we ate lunch at Bogey's, where 50 feet of windows look out onto the course. Pleasant appetizers, nice salads, and
some very good entrees, such as crab-stuffed crab, crab cakes, chicken
and mushroom fettuccine, and Yankee pot roast are served. Both days
we were pleased with the service, the prices, the decor, the food ... what
are we missing here, anything? Nope. It's a very handy place to eat before
or after a round on this course. Between the kitchen and the course,
Riverside is a favorite of outings, so a call to make sure there's room is a
good idea.

The course starts with a long, straight par 5 of 560 yards from the whites. It's the number one handicap, and we wondered if its resistance to par was a matter of players not being warmed up. (Not to get off the subject, but we were talking last year with Sandy Davis, the teacher at Hilliard Lakes, and it's her opinion that we often lose as many as five strokes when we often fail to warm up properly.)

No. 9 is no pushover either, warmed up or not. A dogleg right, it's 414 yards long and the number three handicap.

The back side is more of the same, including No. 17, a touch par 4 of 410 yards.

ACCOMMODATIONS

Edinboro Inn   (814) 734-5650
401 West Plum St., Edinboro, PA

ROOMS: 105; **SUITES:** 6

ROOM RATES: $55–$95   **PAYMENT:** checks, MC, VS, AX, DIS, DC

SPECIAL RATES: AAA

RESTAURANTS: Gardenia (avg. entree $9)

RESORT AMENITIES: cable TV/movies

CONFERENCE/BUSINESS MEETING FACILITIES: banquet and meeting facilities that overlook the golf course available

GOLF

COURSES:

Culbertson Hills Golf Resort   (814) 734-3114
SR 6N, Edinboro, PA

Riverside Golf Club   (814) 398-4692
24527 Rte. 19, Cambridge Springs, PA

OTHER ATTRACTIONS NEARBY

Waldameer Park, Conneaut Lake & Park, Conneaut Cellars winery, Campbell's Pottery, Edinboro University

DIRECTIONS

I-90 east; south on I-79 to exit 166 for Edinboro; north on SR-6.

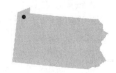

FARMINGTON, PA
NEMACOLIN WOODLANDS & MYSTIC ROCK

The resort? A slice of heaven.
The golf? A devil of a course.

LOCATION: Southwest PA
DRIVE TIME: 4–5 hours
COST: $$$

....

STAY: Nemacolin Woodlands Resort & Spa, Farmington, PA
PLAY: Mystic Rock Golf Course, Farmington, PA

Maybe Nemacolin Woodlands Resort isn't the Eighth Wonder of the World. But if we stretch the list to nine or ten ... If there is a heaven, Nemacolin is an excellent introduction to the delights. And if there isn't, this might do for most golfers. Whether one believes in an afterlife or not, to pass from this earth without spending some time at Nemacolin would be a shame.

Nemacolin is far more than a resort, though the resort amenities are magnificent. It is a living museum that constantly delights and awakens the senses, including intellectual. It is a pulsating testament to Joe Hardy, the guy with the plainest name, biggest dreams, and most remarkable appreciation for the joys of life and sharing them.

With 275 guest rooms, suites, and townhouses, this Laurel Highlands resort offers 36 holes of golf (yes, Tiger played here), 30 stations for sporting clays, an equestrian center and polo field, more than a dozen specialty shops, a private airstrip (yes, President Clinton landed here), a magnificent spa, and an art collection so large and so varied a 180-page book was published describing it. The artwork is accessible: guests can relax in the library under a Louis Tiffany lamp shade, stand under a Calder mobile, and see one of Marilyn Monroe's dresses—a sleek little black number—hanging on a wall.

A leisurely stroll through the resort yields delightful discoveries. A huge free-standing cylindrical salt water aquarium is here, filled with fish from the Red Sea, the Caribbean, and the oceans off Hawaii and

Florida. It stands twelve feet high and contains 8,500 gallons of salt water. On the bottom rests a "finger of gold," a gold bar lost when the Spanish galleon *Santa Margarita* ran aground and split in a hurricane. The year was 1622.

A full-size bronze sculpture of Mark Twain sits on a park bench. The front end of a 1950 Cadillac pokes through a hallway wall. Another bronze, this one of Gene Sarazen in knickers and necktie, stands, leaning on a wood, at one of the tees on Mystic Rock.

Not that anyone is counting, but there are more places to enjoy dining here than on most cruise ships. Lautrec is Nemacolin's homage to contemporary French, and for gentlemen, jackets are requested though not required. It is here the wine cellar plays an important role and the menu features wood-roasted antelope, San Francisco Bay cioppino, and Togarashi-seared tuna. Soups and desserts are to die for.

Seasons, at the spa, is what great nutrition can taste like in the hands of the right chef. The Golden Trout is casual, and on the menu is roasted top round leg of lamb, chargrilled beef tenderloin, and its signature pan-roasted golden trout. There are a few taverns, bars, and lounges, as well as the Tea Room, where traditional English tea is served along with pastries. Resident pianist Jace plays the classics.

The Woodlands Spa was renovated and reopened in May of 1999. Owners Joe Hardy and Maggie Hardy Magerko spent $14 million on the project. The facility has 32,000 square feet filled with 28 treatment rooms, a 2,400-square-foot fitness center, a full service salon, and a swimming pool.

While we were at Nemacolin, a Cleveland law firm was there, too. The Business Center here provides everything from secretarial service to audio/visual equipment, as well as meeting rooms of varying sizes. There is also a workstation for those who just cannot, under any circumstances, leave work behind; it has a PC with internet access, laser printer, fax machine, and copier, and is available 24/7.

THE GOLF

Guests here can have a great time without ever stepping up to the first tee, but passing up Mystic Rock would be difficult for any golfer. While this story is apocryphal, it's worth retelling. Designer Pete Dye, when

DYE DIDN'T MOVE GIANT BOULDERS IF HE DIDN'T HAVE TO OR IF THEY ADDED VALUE TO HIS DESIGN

hired, toured the property then reported back to owner Joe Hardy. Dye said it was a gorgeous piece of land, but there was no way a golf course could be laid out—too many boulders; the expense would be prohibitive. How much, Hardy asked? A million and a half per hole, Dye said. Can you start tomorrow? Hardy inquired.

Whatever the price, Dye clearly enjoyed himself as he created a course that will last for many generations. (By the way, did we tell you that the course was named by an employee? True. There was a contest among the help, and Mystic Rock was selected.)

Playing Mystic Rock once is exciting, playing it twice is fascinating, playing it the third time allows observant players to see more of what Dye demands in order to score well. And playing it a fourth time from the championship tees where Tiger Woods hit from suddenly gives a new understanding of just how good Woods is!

From a purely aesthetic view, the course is memorable. Dye didn't move giant boulders if he didn't have to. He used many to add value to his design. To the giant boulders, he added giant bunkers and greens that show new subtleties with every round. It stretches out to 6,832 yards, par 72. The course rating is 75.0, so don't plan on setting the course record, and the slope is 146.

The links course was built first. It measures 6,643 yards and is no pushover, but it is more peaceful than its younger brother—par is 71, the course rating is 73.0, and the slope is 131. The Links takes a languorous canter through the Highlands, and has water, tough rough, and handsome stands of hardwoods.

ACCOMMODATIONS

Nemacolin Woodlands Resort & Spa   (800) 422-2736
1001 Lafayete Dr., Farmington, PA

ROOMS: 196; **SUITES:** 79

ROOM RATES: $250–$3,000   **PAYMENT:** checks, MC, VS, AX, DIS, DC

SPECIAL RATES: AAA

RESTAURANTS: Lautrec (avg. entree $31), Golden Trout ($19), Seasons ($20), Caddy Shack ($16), The Tavern ($11)

RESORT AMENITIES: indoor pool, outdoor pool, health club, sauna, hot tub, cable TV/movies, room service, smoking rooms, non-smoking rooms, babysitting service, conference facilities, full-service spa, sporting clays, equestrian center, retail shops, art collection, airstrip, youth programs, hiking, biking, fly fishing

CONFERENCE/BUSINESS MEETING FACILITIES: meeting and banquet areas available that accommodate up to 900 people; meeting packages are available

SPECIAL PROGRAMS FOR CHILDREN: full- and half-days of supervised entertainment for children 4 to 9; "kids night out" for kids 4 to 12; teen scene for kids 13 to 17

GOLF

GOLF PACKAGE RATES: $165–$606 for 1 day and 1 round

PACKAGE INCLUDES: cart rental; weekend packages available; Sun–Thu packages available

COURSE:

Mystic Rock Golf Course   (800) 422-2736
1001 LaFayette Dr., Farmington, PA

OTHER ATTRACTIONS NEARBY

Fallingwater, Kentuck Knob, Laurel Caverns, Ft. Necessity National Battlefield, antiques shopping

DIRECTIONS

I-80 east; east on to PA Turnpike; south on SR-119 to New Stanton exit; east on SR-40 east; on left.

GIBSONIA, PA
SUN & CRICKET
& DEER RUN

*For outdoorsy folks seeking
privacy and pampering*

LOCATION: Western PA
DRIVE TIME: 3–4 hours
COST: $
....
STAY: Sun & Cricket Bed and
Breakfast, Gibsonia, PA
PLAY: Deer Run Golf Club,
Gibsonia, PA
NEARBY: downtown Pittsburgh

Over all the miles and all the rooms and all the restaurants and golf courses we visited for this book, a few were so nice, so inviting, so pleasurable that we really didn't want to leave. We promised ourselves we would return. Sun & Cricket Bed and Breakfast is such a place.

It was built by John Bradley-Steck and his wife, Tara, who said simply, "This is a restful retreat." It is more than that. It is the slowly fashioned dream of a husband and wife who sought beauty and, discovering it, offered to share it.

The property consists of 35 acres of old farmland and woods purchased in 1982. What the Bradley-Stecks wanted to do was build a home for themselves. Over the first two years, that's what they did with a log cabin (it would someday become one of the B & B suites). The next construction project was a barn. They found an existing one about five miles from their home built in 1803 of planks of chestnut. Next to it sat an old dance hall. They purchased both and began dismantling them for the move to the Bradley-Steck property.

As the barn and adjoining carriage house went up, the Bradley-Stecks wondered about a B & B. When Tara traveled on business, she preferred to stay in B & Bs. In fact, she knew a lot about them, having stayed in more than 200 over the years.

As they talked about the possibilities, the responsibility for the interiors and decorating settled on Tara's shoulders, and the outside work and duties landed on John's. The business venture meant building a home for

themselves and using what they already had for guests.

There are only two suites at Sun & Cricket. The one-room Carriage House, 500 feet from the main house, sleeps up to three. It is right next to the barn. If this structure isn't the inspiration for most covers of Country Living, we'll be hornswoggled. Although the unit has a great list of amenities (gas logs, small refrigerator, microwave, coffee maker, stereo TV, VCR, a full bath, queen-size bed, air conditioning, and a skylight), it doesn't have telephone service. A weekend without a phone.

The barn, right next door, is home to four horses, a pair of sheep (Champ and Sparkle), and a couple barn swallow families. By the way, you're welcome to bring Old Dobbin out and ride his swayback butt up and down the bridle trails here. There is a separate corral for him.

The other suite is the log cabin, and it sleeps as many as four. It's attached to the main house where John and Tara live, so late at night keep it down to a mild roar.

One of many striking details in the log cabin is the three-story spiral staircase. There are beds on the first and third floors, and the main level features a large living room, wood-burning fireplace, air conditioning, an atrium with floor-to-ceiling windows, a small library of books and tapes, TV, VCR, and the dreaded telephone for those who mistakenly think life can't go on without them.

In addition to the bridle trails, there are wonderful hiking trails that wend through gorgeous countryside, and nearby are antiques shops and outstanding restaurants. And as Tara pointed out, "With just two suites, it doesn't get that busy."

We stayed in the carriage house, and when first light slipped through the skylight, we pulled the blinds open. The horses stood there, mute testimony to this most relaxing, most elegant B & B. The breakfast was wonderful, too.

Eventually we had to leave Sun and Cricket and go play golf. Tough job, we agreed, but someone has to do it. Plus, with the way we filled up at the breakfast table, a little walking would do us good.

THE GOLF

We were lucky picking a course. There are a number nearby, and Deer Run Golf Club is a semi-private track only five minutes away. We loved what owner Fran Magister said about running her course, which opened in 1984, "You can never sit on your laurels. Every year you have to present something new or better than you had the year before. Adding tees, new hazards, and slight changes in the hole configurations are examples. This year flower beds were added."

Deer Run has bent grass tees, fairways, and greens. Much of the woods were kept intact and used by designer Ron Forse, who also had some western Pennsylvania mountain terrain to incorporate.

We wondered which holes would stand out as signature holes, but you know what? Every darn one of them could qualify. Forse tucked some greens into wooded alcoves, had others at the end of downhill rides, and still others that dance along the edge of ravines. He had great property to work with, and he did very, very well.

There are four sets of tees here, and they are notably distant from one another. The blues are 7,066 yards, whites are 6,345, gold is 5,847, and red is 5,255, still a long course for most players comfortable at the forward tees.

It was on No. 5, a 392-yard par 4, that we remembered our course management lectures. Trees guard the right side here, and a good drive offers an elevated view of the green, well trapped and bordered with trees on the right side. Getting on here in regulation, we decided, meant a player was warmed up, swinging and playing well. The next hole, a 164-yard par 3, had a ravine on the right side, and who knows how many dozen Titleists resting at the bottom.

The front nine was a delight, and the back nine was more challenging.

SOME GREENS TUCK INTO WOODEN ALCOVES; SOME DANCE ALONG THE EDGE OF RAVINES.

Beginning with No. 10, a 490-yard par 5, with the fairway canting right, and woods lining both sides. The proper landing area is left, and a narrow fairway leads players, flanked by sand and trees and a ravenous ravine, to the green. Overhitting the approach means the ball tumbling downhill.

One of many great holes was No. 11, a 382-yard par 4 that slopes to a creek on the right and pond in front of the green, and surprise, a covered bridge leading to the green.

Now where's that darn camera?

ACCOMMODATIONS

Sun & Cricket Bed and Breakfast   (724) 444-6300
1 Tara Lane, Gibsonia, PA

SUITES: 2

ROOM RATES: $105–$125   **PAYMENT:** checks, MC, VS, AX, DIS

SPECIAL RATES: $10/night discount for stays of 2 nights or more

RESTAURANTS: Sun & Cricket offers full breakfast

RESORT AMENITIES: outdoor pool, fireplaces in rooms, private entrances, in-room massages, hiking trails

CONFERENCE/BUSINESS MEETING FACILITIES: spacious 24x24 room with private entrance

GOLF

COURSE:

Deer Run Golf Club   (724) 265-4800
287 Monier Rd., Gibsonia, PA

OTHER ATTRACTIONS NEARBY

Pittsburgh (Pirates, Steelers, Penguins); Hartwood Acres Park (free summer concerts, hiking trails); Deer Lake Park (fishing, nature trails); Beechwood Farms Park (Audubon Society park, bird sanctuary); Salon Vivace Day Spa, Tour-ed Mine, antique and outlet shopping

DIRECTIONS

I-80 east; east on I-76 to exit 4; north on SR-8; east on the Red Belt (Barberstown-Warrendale Rd.); right on Tara Ln.

HIDDEN VALLEY, PA
HIDDEN VALLEY FOUR SEASONS RESORT

A luxurious yet family-centered getaway

LOCATION: Southwest PA
DRIVE TIME: 3–4 hours
COST: $$
....
STAY: Hidden Valley Four Seasons Resort, Hidden Valley, PA
PLAY: Hidden Valley Golf Course, Hidden Valley, PA
NEARBY: Idlewild Park

We like this place. A lot. Not just for its food, lodging, incredible views of the Laurel Highlands, or its business center, which is full conference facilities. (So nice, in fact, we sometimes wish we had real jobs, and our real companies would go to places like this and take us along!) Each of these is important, but it was the people who work here that made it wonderful. They made us so comfortable. Is that because it's a family-centered resort? Whatever the reason, we like this place. If you think pizza and bunk beds when we say "family-centered," excuse us. Hidden Valley is luxurious, as well.

In the 1960s, it opened as a ski resort. In 1984, the Kettler Brothers bought the place and added golf, swimming, tennis, and other activities in an effort to make it a year-round operation. They succeeded.

The Inn and Conference Center is in the original ski lodge; accommodations are private entrance condos, townhouses, or single-family homes. The options include studios and suites all the way to three-bedroom condos and 3- and 4-bedroom homes. Outside the Inn are miles of winding roads up the mountain. They lead to the housing as well as the golf course, which is built on top.

We stayed at a two-bedroom, two-bath condo near the golf course. It had a fully-equipped kitchen (which is one more dining option), large dining area, and living room with sleeper sofa. There was a washer/dryer, coffee maker (with coffee), dishwasher (with soap), and all the towels and linens we could use. We also received standard hotel maid service.

All this fresh air makes us hungry, and the options for food are as numerous as the room amenities: the Hearthside Restaurant is at the Inn and has paneled walls and a huge fireplace. While it is the dressiest of the dining rooms, it's not stuffy. Nice menu, good prices, very good service.

It also serves a Sunday brunch, a daily breakfast, and, on Fridays, a seafood buffet.

Also at the Inn is the Snowshoe Lounge, which offers lighter fare in a more casual atmosphere, a cozy fireplace, TVs hanging in every corner, a pool table, a juke box, and live entertainment on Saturday nights.

Mulligan's Bar & Grill at the golf club serves breakfast and lunch.

THE GOLF

Russell Roberts designed this course, and we can only guess how much he enjoyed coming to work every day. There are a lot of spectacular vistas here, and Roberts knew that when he went to work. On a clear day, you can see as far as 30 miles.

We love his opening hole—a dramatic par 4 that tumbles downhill for a couple hundred yards before turning right, over some water, to the green. There is enough sand and water on the course to get the attention of players, but the water is often aesthetic rather than problematic. Sand often is used to slow or stop errant shots.

The blues are 6,589 yards and the slope is 142. That's 142 reasons to play the whites, which are 6,117 yards and a slope of 136. Look, the golf here is not just gorgeous but very, very challenging.

Fairways are lined with dense forest, and it isn't until the fourth tee that another hole can be seen, and then it's only the No. 8 green. Great drainage, if you need it. Quick greens.

The signature on the back is No. 12, primarily for its view from the tee box. But as we said while playing, if you don't think the view before you is spectacular, turn around and look.

Anyway, No. 12 is 433 yards from the blues, 402 from the whites. It runs downhill until 150 yards from the green, and then it drops severely. We liked the time and money spent on No. 15, a great little uphill par 3 with a stone-lined brook babbling (what else?) down the right side until it decides to cross the fairway.

Because the course is laid out on a summit 2,800 feet above sea level, fog and frost can delay the first tee times. What a great place to sit and wait.

On Nos. 14 and 15, a wildlife refuge borders the course. Last year, a doe gave birth to an albino fawn that was roaming the course. We stopped once to listen to elk calling, and other players spoke of seeing fox, buffalo, elk, and bear in the preserve.

ACCOMMODATIONS

Hidden Valley Four Seasons Resort   (814) 443-8000
One Craighead Drive, Hidden Valley, PA

ROOMS: 128

ROOM RATES: $85–$120   **PAYMENT:** checks, MC, VS, AX, DIS

RESTAURANTS: Snowshoe Lounge (avg. entree $15)

RESORT AMENITIES: indoor pool, outdoor pool, health club, sauna, hot tub, cable TV/movies, smoking rooms, non-smoking rooms, babysitting service, conference facilities

CONFERENCE/BUSINESS MEETING FACILITIES: can accommodate meetings and seminars

GOLF

GOLF PACKAGE RATES: $79–$209 for 1–3 days and unlimited rounds

PACKAGE INCLUDES: cart rental

COURSE:

Hidden Valley Golf Course   (814) 443-8444
One Craighead Dr., Hidden Valley, PA

OTHER ATTRACTIONS NEARBY

CaddieShak Family Fun Park, Idlewild Park, historic Ligonier, Johnstown Flood Museum, Somerset Historical Center, Frick Art Museum

DIRECTIONS

I-80 east; east on I-76; east on I-70 to Somerset Interchange (PA-219) to Johnstown; right on N. Center Ave.; right on Craighead Dr.

IF YOU DON'T THINK THE VIEW BEFORE YOU IS SPECTACULAR, TURN AROUND.

162

MEADVILLE, PA
WHISPERING PINES & OAKLAND BEACH

*A no-nonsense getaway
for no-nonsense golf*

LOCATION: Northwest PA
DRIVE TIME: 2–3 hours
COST: $$

....

STAY: Days Inn Conference Center, Meadville, PA
PLAY: Whispering Pines, Meadville, PA
Oakland Beach Golf Course, Conneaut Lake, PA

Know what we like about Meadville? A lot of things, but mostly we like the fact that it's a semi-small town that's accessible. What do you want to do? You can walk to it. We took our first-born, a sturdy four-year-old, and for him, it was a wonderful adventure. We stayed in the Days Inn, which is right in the middle of town. Highways as well as a host of courses are easily accessible.

Generally, we find Days Inns to be no-nonsense shelters. Everything we need is there, and in most cases, the staff appears to be happy to have guests. That's the way it was here. Our room had a pair of very firm double beds and the important things—a hair dryer and coffee machine—were provided. The 27-inch television screen kept the little guy fascinated before dinner.

Our mother-in-law gave us great advice for taking The Heir to a restaurant: limit the choices, she said. If the little guy can't read, he doesn't know he has two dozen selections. Instead, she counseled, say to him, "Buddy-boy, what do you want for supper? A nice pork chop or some fish?"

We tried pork chops ourselves, along with a plate of chicken Parmesan. Good choices and good service. We gained fresh appreciation for food while doing the back-breaking, thankless, tortuous research for this guide. Bad food or food poorly prepared casts a pall on the weekend. Same with bad service. So we do our part to make food a pleasant, if not memorable, part of the trip.

OTHER STATES : PENNSYLVANIA

When on the road, the art of eating well is a matter of two ideas. First, go hungry. That means passing up the snack bar at the course. When we're hungry, we anticipate the pleasures of eating. It gets us in the mood, if you catch our drift. Second, go with what the locals eat and enjoy.

THE GOLF

Whispering Pines is playable, well conditioned and maintained, and blessed with fast greens and two great par 5s.

The blues are 6,226 yards, par 72. The whites are 5,872 and par 71. No. 12 is a 490-yard par 5 on the blues, but a 401-yard par 4 on the whites. The gold tees are 5,175, and the reds are 4,910 yards.

No. 12, one of our favorites, is a dogleg left with big water right, two lakes separated by an earthen bridge. At 490 yards, it's a three-shotter for mortals, and that water waits silently for second shots not carefully launched.

And No. 15, the other par 5, is a 550-yard par 5 whose fairway runs uphill, peaks, then tumbles down to a green that is somewhat elevated. Most of the greens slope back to front, so pin position can mean a lot here. Leaving the ball above the flag, combined with the speed of these greens, spells double-bogey.

The handsome clubhouse has a bar and grill with a big-screen TV. There is room for five or six dozen customers, and the day we played, the Browns were thumping the Steelers, to the disbelief and dismay of the crowd.

We found a kindred spirit in general manager Carol Kingzett, who was busy replacing beer kegs, cleaning tables, and caring for customers; she is from Lyndhurst. Her father, the owner, bought the place when it was put on the market. It needed some repairs, and his business was contracting. A very good match.

We also played Oakland Beach Golf Club in nearby Conneaut Lake. Another very playable course, Oakland stretched out a little longer at 6,783 from the blues, 6,139 from the whites, and 5,192 for the reds (the perfect length, we think, for the forward tees).

Pace of play is important here, thanks to enlightened management. That doesn't mean the course always plays fast, only that management tries. What it calls the basic principles of "ready golf" are listed on the scorecard, and the first one is: "the player (on the tee) who is ready should hit." That's a variation on our own West Side Honors, which calls for the same procedure. Not to make too fine a point of it, but WSH works only if all players are familiar with the course. Having to hit first on an unfamiliar tee can be unnerving for some.

Three big par 4s get the game underway: No. 3 is 393 yards, No. 4 is 433, and No. 5 is 438. And the front side's second par 5 is No. 7, a 570-yard hole. The yardage markers can throw off the unfamiliar. The blue markers are 200 yards, the red are 150, and the yellow are 100.

ACCOMMODATIONS

Days Inn Conference Center   (814) 337-4264
18360 Conneaut Lake Rd., Meadville, PA

ROOMS: 163

ROOM RATES: $70–$92   **PAYMENT:** checks, MC, VS, AX, DIS, DC

SPECIAL RATES: 10% discount for seniors and AAA

RESTAURANTS: Davenports Restaurant (avg. entree $10.95), Referees Sports Bar & Lounge

RESORT AMENITIES: complimentary Continental breakfast weekdays, indoor pool, hot tub, cable TV/movies, room service, pets welcome, smoking rooms, non-smoking rooms, conference facilities

CONFERENCE/BUSINESS MEETING FACILITIES: hospitality rooms and banquet facilities for up to 400 people.

GOLF

GOLF PACKAGE RATES: from $59.99/person based on double occupancy for 1 day and 1 round

PACKAGE INCLUDES: food/beverages, cart rental; weekend packages available; Sun–Thu packages available

COURSES:

Whispering Pines   (814) 333-2827
15630 Middle Rd., Meadville, PA

Oakland Beach Golf Course   (814) 382-5665
11866 Oakland Beach Rd., Conneaut Lake, PA

DIRECTIONS

I-90 east; south on I-79 to exit 147A for Meadville; on left.

TITUSVILLE, PA
CROSS CREEK
RESORT

*Generous getaway packages at
this vintage 1950s resort*

LOCATION: Northwest PA
DRIVE TIME: 2–3 hours
COST: $$

STAY: Cross Creek Resort, Titusville, PA
PLAY: Cross Creek Golf Course,
Titusville, PA
NEARBY: Pymatuning State Park

Nestled in the rolling hills of western Pennsylvania between sleepy Victorian towns known for their roles in the petroleum industry is an unusual golf resort.

While Curtis Strange honeymooned here (due to a tournament!), it is more a spot to rendezvous with a bunch of buddies or couples for a weekend of rounds on the 27-hole course. Don't look for much else to do here; golf is the thing, and the generous getaway packages reflect that.

Motel-style outbuildings cluster around the perimeter of the property. Rooms are big enough to take full swings in with regulation-length drivers. Ours had two big sleeping rooms, each with queen-sized beds and televisions, one serviceable bathroom, a refrigerator, and small dining area.

The clubhouse is vintage 1950s, an imposing cement block structure with huge picture windows overlooking an outdoor pool, the gorgeous countryside, and, of course, the course. This is the hub for activity. Breakfast, lunch, and dinner are served in a spacious dining room or on an enclosed veranda. Buffet-style meals are included with the packages, or you can order off the menu. Meals are hearty, cuisine that is easy to make well; steaks, veal, fish, and spaghetti are mainstays, and Sunday brunch was more than noteworthy—it was terrific. Go there hungry. (We should mention Cross Creek is also the place for social events and occasions. The one night we stayed, there were three major events happening. This might affect reservations, so make yours accordingly.)

The 19th Hole was another delightful surprise. Accommodating bartenders, a nice menu of light meals, and a lot of sports programming on the television. The ushers from a bridal party were there, oddly elegant in their formal wear, hunkered down in front of a college football game. The 19th Hole is one of two bars on the premises; the other sits atop the clubhouse. In that one, Monday Night Football and other occasions are celebrated, usually with live music.

The decor is wonderfully forgettable; the course is wonderfully memorable.

THE GOLF

Twenty-seven holes make up the course here, the first 18, known as the North Course, was created in the 1940s; the 9-hole South Course was added later. The pro shop staff was impressive, the locker room was spacious and included a big screen television and a lot of couches. The big practice green includes a practice bunker and the driving range ... well, you don't come here to practice, you come here to play.

This is hilltop golf, and it takes well-placed tee shots to avoid sidehill lies. Wind can be a factor here, though as they say in Scotland, "nae wind, nae golf."

The entire course is very well conditioned and maintained. Greens are true and a little on the fast side. While the fraternal similarities between North and South are clear, they offer distinctions, as well.

The North is a "grip and rip" player's dream, with rolling, wide-open fairways and playable rough. Trees separate the fairways, and there is no underbrush. The only water on the North is for drinking. Finishing with the ball you started with is easy. It is 6,166 yards from the whites, 6,467 from the blues.

That doesn't mean scoring well is easy. The greens are well guarded by steep-sided bunkers that wrap around the fronts and sides.

One of the prettiest holes (it figures that it's on the cover of the score-card) is No. 3, a par-three that begins at a cliffside tee box and floats over a pond en route to a well-bunkered green.

Another memorable tee is No. 10, a par-four of 445 yards that leaves the very scenic tee box and slopes downhill. It is a gentle dogleg left that calls for a 230-yard drive to have a clear approach. Though the second shot is downhill, the fairway rises in front of the green, making all the shots carry.

The South is a change of pace. Set into the woods, if features tighter fairways and water that comes into play, but nary a bunker.

No. 2, a par-four of only 370 yards, has water left and a quarrelsome tree to the right of the landing area. Accuracy spoken on this tee. No. 7, another short par-four, this one 357 yards, begins with an uphill, blind tee shot. The fairway slopes down, but players have to negotiate the creek in front of the green. Maybe you'd like to try a Trevino fade to catch the slope of the hill. It will leave a short pitch to the green. But trees and dense woods on the left provide the risk on this risk-and-reward tee.

THE NORTH IS A "GRIP AND RIP" PLAYER'S DREAM.

ACCOMMODATIONS

Cross Creek Resort   (800) 461-3173
3815 State Rte. 8, Titusville, PA

ROOMS: 94; **SUITES:** 8

ROOM RATES: $120–$155   **PAYMENT:** checks, MC, VS, AX, DIS, DC

RESTAURANTS: Fairway (avg. entree $14), Terrace on the Green, The 19th Hole

RESORT AMENITIES: outdoor pool, cable TV/movies, smoking rooms, non-smoking rooms, conference facilities

CONFERENCE/BUSINESS MEETING FACILITIES: can accommodate meetings and seminars

GOLF

GOLF PACKAGE RATES: $175–$450 for 2–4 days and unlimited rounds

PACKAGE INCLUDES: food/beverages, cart rental; weekend packages available; Sun–Thu packages available

COURSE:

Cross Creek Golf Course   (800) 461-3173
Rte. 8, Titusville, PA

OTHER ATTRACTIONS NEARBY

Drake Well Museum, Oil Creek & Titusville Railroad, Pymatuning State Park, Oil Creek State Park, Presque Isle State Park

DIRECTIONS

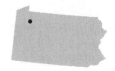

I-80 east; east on PA Turnpike to exit 3 for Barkeyville; north on SR-8 to Franklin Rd.; north on SR-417 to Cherrytree; left on SR-8; on left.

WARREN, PA
BLUEBERRY HILL
& JACKSON VALLEY

Scenery delights on these courses
nestled in the Allegheny Mountains

LOCATION: Northwest PA
DRIVE TIME: 2–3 hours
COST: $

....

STAY: Holiday Inn, Warren, PA
PLAY: Blueberry Hill Golf Course, Russell, PA
Jackson Valley Country Club, Warren, PA
NEARBY: Allegheny National Forest

First things first: it's Warren, PA, not Warren, OH. This Warren is surrounded by the Allegheny Mountains, and the Allegheny River winds through the center of town. (You can canoe it.)

Its economic backbone for the first couple of centuries was lumber, oil, and steel. As the manufacturing climate changed, the area developed as a tourist destination, a very good one.

The Allegheny National Forest is here in all its natural splendor, and the Kinzua Dam Reservoir is a good example of what the Corps of Engineers can do when it feels like damming a river. Boating and fishing are said to be first rate.

The handsome small town has the Struthers Library Theater Summer Playhouse, which does a good job with classic Broadway shows such as *West Side Story* and *Oklahoma*. This is not a group of high-school kids being directed by their maiden aunts, we found out. Starting its 17th season this year, this is a professional theater with very good prices. And if you think shopping the outlet malls in Myrtle Beach is fun, you'll probably spend some time at Blair Outlet and Retail Store.

The Holiday Inn puts together golf packages at four courses: Blueberry Hill GC, Jackson Valley GC, Pine Acres GC, and Cable Hollow GC. Rooms (there are 110 of them) at the Inn have more than the average golfer needs: hair dryer, iron and ironing board in the room, and just down the hall are indoor pool, sauna, and exercise room.

Also just down the hall is the redoubtable Tootsie's Restaurant and Lounge. The menu includes lamb, beef, pasta, and seafood, including lobster. Kids under 18 can stay and eat without charge.

One advantage of staying at a Holiday Inn is knowing it'll be good. The rooms will be properly equipped, the staff will be professional, and the food and drink will be first rate.

THE GOLF

Blueberry Hill GC is the sort of course that gets us excited. It is 2,300 feet above sea level, nestled in the Allegheny Mountains. Because of the elevation, it's usually the last course in the area to open, but it's worth the wait.

We are walk-and-carry players—the Izzo double-strap bag comfortably settled across our shoulders—and Blueberry is a walkers' course.

Designed by James Harrison and Ferdinand Garbin, the course opened its first nine in 1961 and the second in 1970.

It is not short: from the back of the box, it's 6,716 yards. From the whites, it's still long, at 6,428. Red tees play at 5,813. There is a fourth set of tees.

At the pro shop we picked up a guide to the course written by pro Jill Jerauld. She describes the holes and tells you how each one should be played. Then it's a matter of adjusting her advice to your game.

Walking when playing is often its own reward, but coming up to the tee box at No. 6 is an additional treat. It's the signature hole—a great par 4 measuring a little more than 400 yards. The tee shot is essentially uphill to a blind landing area, and from there it goes right. It's O.B. on the left and woods on the right.

We took a minute to enjoy the view from the landing area. When you look back, you're looking out for more than 50 miles. Gorgeous!

Jackson Valley Country Club, another course in the Alleghenies needs more than one round to be fully enjoyed.

The Jackson Run Creek has a presence on eight holes, and two additional holes have water hazards. The only way to get in trouble is to be wild. If you can find the fairways, it's rewarding.

The course begins with a short par 5 of 449 yards. No. 3, the number one handicap, is substantially longer: 546 yards. The first of the par 3s on the front is long, too: 195 yards (hey, it's 230 yards from the blues).

We note that the fairway irrigation system is going in and the cart paths need some work.

ACCOMMODATIONS

Holiday Inn   (800) 446-6814
210 Ludlow St., Warren, PA

ROOMS: 110

ROOM RATES: $65–$85   **PAYMENT:** checks, MC, VS, AX, DIS, DC

SPECIAL RATES: none

RESTAURANTS: Tootsie's Restaurant (avg. entree $13)

RESORT AMENITIES: indoor pool, health club, sauna, cable TV/movies, room service, pets welcome, smoking rooms, non-smoking rooms, conference facilities, garden atrium, nightclub

CONFERENCE/BUSINESS MEETING FACILITIES: two separate conference rooms available for up to 300 guests

SPECIAL PROGRAMS FOR CHILDREN: kids eat free and stay free; board games available at front desk.

GOLF

GOLF PACKAGE RATES: $215/person, double occupancy for 3 days and 3 rounds

PACKAGE INCLUDES: food/beverages, cart rental, all tips; weekend packages available

COURSES:

Blueberry Hill Golf Course   (814) 757-8620
Warren & Onoville Rd., Russell, PA

Jackson Valley Country Club   (814) 489-7802
1947 Jackson Run Rd., Warren, PA

OTHER ATTRACTIONS NEARBY

Kinzua Dam and Reservoir (swimming and boating), Allegheny National Forest (scenic outlooks, hiking, biking), Struthers Library Theater, Blair Outlet

DIRECTIONS

I-90 east to Erie PA; south on SR-19; east on SR-6 to Warren; on corner of Ludlow St. and SR- 6.

WEST MIDDLESEX, PA
YANKEE RUN

If you've never driven a golf cart with a global positioning unit...

The Radisson Hotel Sharon is your typical modern hotel—bright, airy, and spacious—but in 100 of the 153 rooms there are Jacuzzi baths. As sales manager Robert DeLuca says, "It's an easy sell, especially on weekends." There

LOCATION: Western PA
DRIVE TIME: 1–2 hours
COST: $

STAY: Radisson Hotel, West Middlesex, PA
PLAY: Yankee Run Golf Course, Brookfield, OH

are five suites, too. And there is a real emphasis on golf. The hotel has package deals with nine area clubs.

The Crystal Steakhouse, where filets, porterhouses, strips, and top sirloins dominate the menu. The New York strip is far and away the favorite. The chicken marsala is also noteworthy. Service is excellent. JW's Other Club is the less-formal dining room here as well as the name of the lounge.

THE GOLF

Yankee Run has legs. More than 70 years old, it was recently honored by the Ohio Golf Course Owners Association as its Course of the Year. The owners association is not alone in its high regard for Yankee Run; *Golf Digest* awards it four stars on the basis of reader surveys. The National Golf Foundation has presented Yankee Run with its Public Golf Achievement Award. Three times.

Golf Shop Operations magazine named it one of America's best 100 pro shops in 1986 and the Northern Ohio PGA honored it as the 1996 Merchandiser of the Year. For the past two decades, the club's August yard sale has drawn players from New York, Pennsylvania, and Ohio. Prices are wholesale or lower.

This old track started in 1929 when two farms, the Jones Farm and the McMullin Farm, were joined. The course is now in the hands of the third generation. Paul McMullin, PGA, is the pro; brother Gary is the greens superintendent.

Their grand uncle, Bill Jones, got things rolling. A student at Cornell, he came home to announce that golf was being played in Ithaca, New York, and it might be a good idea to create a course here. Unable to foresee the Depression, he could not have had worse timing. A mechanical engineer, he laid out the first nine holes. When the McMullin's fathers and uncles returned form World War II, they built the second nine; it opened in 1947.

It plays 6,501 yards, par 70, from the blue tees and 6,103 from the whites. The red tees are the perfect length: 5,140 yards, par 73. It is fully watered and very well conditioned. The clubhouse first served as a horse barn. It has been remodeled and expanded three times. So far. It is one of the few public tracks that offers locker rooms for men and women.

Play begins par 5, par 3, par 5, and at that point players unfamiliar with the course will have a good idea of the many pleasures and challenges that await. No. 1 is a 496-yard par 5 with the real challenge at the green, which is elevated. No. 2 is a long, 172-yard par 3 that plays longer because it's uphill, and the third hole is another par 5, this one a big, curving fairway stretching 561 yards.

Playing the par 3s here in par means a very good round. For the other two par 3s on the front side, hitting the green is vital. Both Nos. 6 and 8 have gullies in front of the green, and missing long or left on No. 6 means trouble. The slope, back to front, on No. 8 can generously be called brutal.

On the back side, there is only one par 5, No. 16, which is 491 yards softly turning right. The course records for blue and white tees are the same: 63. Oak Tree pro Jerry McGee, from East Liverpool, played in a grocer's outing and even with a bogey shot 63.

THE SLOPE ON NO. 8 CAN GENEROUSLY BE CALLED BRUTAL

It's the short game here that is important. Many clubs refer to their courses as being shotmakers' tracks, but Yankee Run really is.

Carts are outfitted with global positioning units. Not only can you see where you stand in an outing, but you can order food to be picked up when you make the turn. Checking the yardage is now as simple as looking at a screen. The owners love it because it allows them to be 'nice' rangers. Paul McMullin says, "One of the difficult situations in golf is slow play and the rangers who try to speed it up. They're often too timid or so abusive they drive customers away. With this, I can tell slow players they're behind and offer assistance."

ACCOMMODATIONS

Radisson Hotel   (724) 528-2501
Route 18 & 1-80, West Middlesex, PA

ROOMS: 153; **SUITES:** 5

ROOM RATES: $69–$159   **PAYMENT:** checks, MC, VS, AX, DIS, DC

RESTAURANTS: Crystal Steakhouse (avg. entree $16), JW's Other Club (avg. entree $10)

RESORT AMENITIES: indoor pool, health club, sauna, hot tub, cable TV/movies, room service, pets welcome, smoking rooms, non-smoking rooms, conference facilities

CONFERENCE/BUSINESS MEETING FACILITIES: five meeting rooms accommodating 8–50, two executive board rooms with AV equipment, and a ballroom that accommodates up to 500

GOLF

GOLF PACKAGE RATES: $87–$227 for 1–4 days and 1–4 rounds

PACKAGE INCLUDES: food/beverages, cart rental; weekend packages available;
Sun–Thu packages available

COURSE:

Yankee Run Golf Course   (800) 446-5346
7610 Sharon Warren Rd., Brookfield, OH

OTHER ATTRACTIONS NEARBY

candy factories (Philadelphia Candies & Daffins Candies), antique and outlet shopping, Amish country

DIRECTIONS

I-80 east to exit 1N for Youngstown towards NY; north on SR-60;
south on SR-18; on left.

ZELIENOPLE, PA
INN ON GRANDVIEW
& OLDE STONEWALL

*What do you get when you cross
a B&B with a castle?*

LOCATION: Western PA

DRIVE TIME: 2–3 hours

COST: $$

....

STAY: The Inn on Grandview Bed &
Breakfast, Zelienople, PA

PLAY: Olde Stonewall Golf Club,
Ellwood City, PA

NEARBY: downtown Pittsburgh

First we went to Zelieonople, and then we went to Elwood City—small towns close to one another in western Pennsylvania. The bed and breakfast we stayed at in Zelieonople was built in the early 19th century and started life as the Zimmerman Hotel. (There is a Zimmerman Room today), with original beams and bricks are exposed; it features a whirlpool bath, gas fireplace, and queen size four-poster. There are also rooms named Glenn, Heasley, and Eppinger, and each has a history.

The Inn on Grandview (Grandview Avenue) is owned and operated by Juanita and Rich Eppinger. They met on a street corner here in 1953. Rich had just been mustered out of the Army. They were married in 1954 at the church right next door to their inn, St. Peter's Reformed.

As a little girl, Juanita would grab any piece of furniture that was headed to the garbage dump, and, if she could see potential in it, she would salvage, strip, and refinish it. When she was in high school, she learned how to paper walls. And before you know it, she was serving as an interior designer. While it was all word of mouth, among her customers were a few Pittsburgh Steelers (and to judge from the colors on their uniforms, those guys needed all the help they could get) and a Pittsburgh television personality. Juanita's skill and vision allowed her to see what the Inn could look like when Rich and Juanita joined her son, Tim, to purchase the Inn in the early nineties. As the Inn's business grew, she had to sell her design business.

It wasn't an inn then, and neither Rich nor Juanita had ever stayed in a B & B before. "We were just going to have four rooms with shared baths. But the ink wasn't even dry on the purchase agreement when Tim was here tearing the place apart. We dug out the basement, put in new wiring and drywall, built new rooms, and put in a new furnace, new

plumbing, and carpet and siding, too." The work took two years, and this was while no money was coming in from the Inn.

Opening Day was Easter Sunday, 1994, and it was a Washington, D.C. couple who stayed. Juanita never asked how they came to know about the Inn. "They've been back," Juanita said, "and lots of our business is return business."

No surprise to us. The place is a delight, and the breakfast with the hostess is not only a wonderful meal, it's a social gathering.

Ah, breakfast. Blueberries bigger than marbles to plop on the steaming bowl of oatmeal, broiled grapefruit, thick slices of bacon smoked right here in town, yogurt, all sorts of pastries and rolls, tea, and coffee. How do you want your eggs?

"I'm amazed how often people have a great time at the breakfast," the hostess said. "And I've learned more than I ever thought I could."

An example? What are the two states in the U.S. where you can't pump your own gas? New Jersey and Oregon.

Let's see, we had breakfast with Juanita, lunch at Shakespeare's Pub, and dinner at Kaufmann's Restaurant in Zelie. Little wonder we put on a couple pounds this trip.

Enough about this lovely town and the host and hostess at the Inn. The golf on this trip is worthy of note, as well.

THE GOLF

The golf course, another Hurdzan & Fry masterpiece, is called Olde Stonewall Golf Club, and it sits behind Shakespeare's, which is a castle. Not a play castle. You are cruising down Route 65 in Elwood City when suddenly, a huge, gray castle looms on the right.

We pulled open huge, black, beveled glass doors to the lobby. They are antiques from a Pittsburgh church. We half expected Sir John Gielgud to be waiting in doublet and tights, and asking, as he reached for the handle of his sword, "Though I bid thee good morn, sir and wench, tell me whose company you seek and tell me quickly, that I might stay this sword from sampling your blood as its sharp blade silences your reluctant tongues!"

We were met instead by general manager Sean Fitzpatrick, who sat with us for a bit and explained much of the castle and its incredible decor.

In the lobby is "Song of Sixpence," a 1912 original painting by D. C. Lithgow that depicts a medieval feast with court jesters.

Carpets and tapestries throughout were purchased in Spain and India by owner Richard Hvizdak. There are four six-foot tin men, replicas of men in suits of armor. There are swords, shields, and battle ornaments, which are not originals, but authentic replicas throughout. The walls of the castle were made from cross-cut oak, and the grand hall seats 250.

You get the idea, don't you? It is difficult to adequately describe what Hvizdak has created here. Not that there weren't a few townies mad at him for doing something daring and original.

His golf course is more of the same: daring, original, and more exciting than bad brakes. With a piece of property most designers would deem undesignable and a passion for taking the road less traveled, the owner has created a most memorable place for a round of golf.

Olde Stonewall Golf Club has five sets of tees, changes in elevation that go into three figures, a superintendent whose job is likely more challenging than most, and a design team that must love opportunities like this.

It is while we played this up-and-down-and-over-and-around-and-through course that we toasted whoever did the routing. How the heck did they find this course in these steep hills? And how did they design it so it's playable for high handicaps yet still a joy for better players?

It plays 6,944 from the tips, or the Epic tees (as they're called—it goes Epic, Medieval, Stonewall, Feudal, and Rustic), beginning with a par 5 that is tree-lined and has fairway bunkers on both sides. No. 2 is where the course rolls over and wakes up. A par 4 dogleg right of 392 yards, a pot bunker sits in the middle of the fairway as if it didn't know what a psychological hazard it represented. Ha! There is nothing here that hasn't been carefully planned and executed. Nos. 4, 5, and 6 race around water so pretty we forgot it was a hazard. At this point, the course begins its long and exciting journey upward, and the tee boxes and views have to be experienced, not described.

There are so many distinctive holes here, it's tough deciding which to

SUDDENLY, A HUGE, GRAY CASTLE LOOMS ON THE RIGHT.

write about, but Nos. 14 and 16 will always be special to us. No. 14 because this 202-yard par 3 starts from an elevated tee and carries two ponds en route to the green. And No. 16, a par 4 that gives better directions than club pro Jessie Horner. Again, from an elevated tee, the landing area is so clear that to miss it means another victory for attention deficit disorder. Both the drive and the approach will carry water, and the hole bends a bit to the left as it gets closer and closer to this well-bunkered green.

ACCOMMODATIONS

The Inn on Grandview Bed & Breakfast   (888) 544-3481
310 E. Grandview Ave., Zelienople, PA

ROOMS: 4

ROOM RATES: $85–$145   **PAYMENT:** checks, MC, VS, AX, DIS

SPECIAL RATES: reduced rates Sun–Thu

RESTAURANTS: breakfast served at the Inn on Grandview

RESORT AMENITIES: cable TV/movies, fireplaces, whirlpools, phones, A/C

GOLF

COURSE:

Olde Stonewall Golf Club   (724) 752-0577
1551 Mercer Rd., Ellwood City, PA

OTHER ATTRACTIONS NEARBY

Moraine State Park (hiking, fishing, boating), McConnels Mill State Park, Volaat (Amish country), Pittsburgh, historic Harmony and Zelienople, Jennings Environmental Education Center, Fallingwater and Kentuck Knob, antiques shopping, outlet shopping

DIRECTIONS

I-80 east; east on I-76 to exit 3 for SR-19; north on SR-19 to Zelienople; right on Grandview Ave.

BERKELEY SPRINGS, WV
CACAPON RESORT

A real home atmosphere for families

Wé're not going to get in a fight over it, but after a lot of travel we have to say no state is prettier, more dramatic, or more fun than West Virginia. (From a historical perspective, we find the fun part odd, because there are a great many Scots here, and let's face it, they are not a race known for partying.)

LOCATION: Northeast WV
DRIVE TIME: 5–6 hours
COST: $

STAY: Cacapon Resort State Park, Berkeley Springs, WV
PLAY: Cacapon Mountain Golf Course, Berkely Springs, WV

And it is all accessible. Cacapon is one of dozens of state parks in West Virginia. It takes in 6,000 gorgeous acres and stretches from the Virginia border to within a few miles of the Potomac River and West Virginia's northern border with Maryland. Driving there we went through Ohio, Pennsylvania, Maryland, and finally West Virginia. That sounds like a long trip. It isn't. For shun pikers, it's a delight.

There are plenty of great activities for families, and when the activities are hitched to a premier golf course, the place offers a great package.

Three major developments helped create Cacapon. The first was the Civilian Conservation Corps (CCC), a federal program created to ease unemployment during the Depression. The CCC built the original Old Inn, an eleven-room facility with a large dining room and fireplace. Today the Old Inn is down the hill from the main lodge and provides a delightful and unusual spot for meetings or family gatherings.

In the early forties, the CCC effort continued with construction of the bathhouse, beach, picnic areas, stables, cabins, water and sewer systems, superintendent's residence, and lots more. In the 1950s, 11 deluxe cabins were added, along with two more residences. The main lodge followed in 1956 and had 50 rooms and a restaurant. In 1973, the crowning glory—

as far as we're concerned—was delivered: a Robert Trent Jones championship golf course carved into the sides of the Cacapon Mountains.

Want to hold a meeting? The lodge can comfortably accommodate 10 to 200. And the lodge has a homey feel to it—you truly feel like a guest here instead of a customer. The great room, just off the main lobby, has the look and feel of a family room and offers board games (remember them?), a television, and a fireplace. Downstairs, the game room has billiards, ping pong, shuffle board, and video games.

Cacapon superintendent Tom Ambrose said, "This is not a revolving door type of resort complex. I like to think of it as more of a home atmosphere for families."

In addition to the golf, there are 20 miles of hiking and bridle paths, tennis and volleyball courts, boat rentals, and horseback riding. The programs here offer guided hikes, slide shows, crafts workshops, and movies.

Pack a bathing suit; the lake, within walking distance, has a white sand beach and lifeguard on duty. Cacapon guests swim there free.

If you thought, as we did, the name came from a stuttering waiter ordering chicken, you were wrong. Cacapon comes from the Shawnee Indian word for medicine. It refers to the healing waters here. In nearby Berkeley Springs State Park, the springs produce mineral-rich waters that have been enjoyed by uncounted generations of Native Americans. It is America's original spa, and for our money, still one of the best.

One of the better-known customers was George Washington, who started coming here as a teenager while working on a surveying team.

AMERICA'S ORIGINAL SPA, "CACAPON" REFERS TO THE HEALING WATERS The state park has the baths, where we enjoyed Roman baths and massages. Finally, we said while walking out, something government can do well! The Roman bath is nine feet long, five feet wide, and fills to four feet deep. It is 101 degrees Farenheit. It is indescribably delightful, and, yes, the aches and pains of age and arthritis or muscle pulls disappear. Also offered there are steam cabinets and infrared heat.

It's fun to pore over the guest registration book in the lobby. The U.S. is well represented and so is Europe.

THE GOLF

Delightful as Cacapon is, it's the golf course that makes it whole. The course, built in 1974, is laid out on former farmland. It is highly regarded course and listed on several "best-designed courses" lists. It is not exceptionally long: the blues play 6,827, the whites 6,267, the gold 5,910, and the red, 5,647. Well, the red tees are long. The most playable red tees usu-

ally come in around 5,000 yards, so this course will be a challenge for many red-tee players.

The short length doesn't mean it's easy. We played the whites and found a wonderful challenge. Eleven holes have doglegs, some more acute than others. The front nine sets up at the base of Cacapon Mountain, and the holes are relatively level. But on the back nine, the holes start inching up the mountain, and sidehill lies are common. Not severe, but common.

There's a nice clubhouse here, well stocked and attached to a snack bar with an outdoor patio. A driving range and putting green are available. Next to the putting green stands a tall chimney where a century-old cabin once stood. The cabin went—the chimney stayed.

Seventy-two sand bunkers are strategically scattered on this course, and the greens are exceptional. In addition to the easily-seen bumps and boogies, there are hidden breaks here, to the extent we swore at one time that the green was moving as we putted. Other times we swore just for the sheer pleasure of swearing on a golf course.

We're fans of the simple things in golf, one of them being definition between fairway and rough. Not only does it make the course more attractive, it helps the player visualize shots. It's that way here.

Water comes into play only two times: on No. 2, a par 4 of 363 yards and on No. 9, a par 5 of 510 yards.

After a pleasant, 351-yard par 4 opening hole, No. 2 is a 363-yard par 4 with a tight landing area and water to the right and front of the green. The water on No. 9 is to the left of the green.

Holes 4 and 8, both par 3s, share a green—a pleasant design surprise. Losing a shot left on No. 4 means hauling out the hiking boots. No. 8 is not so trouble-laden; a sand bunker guards the front.

The numbers one and two handicap holes are carbon copies of each other; No. 7 is a 408-yard par 4, and No.16 is a 375-yard par 4. Both are doglegs left with sand in the elbow.

No. 11 sounds like an easy par 5, a guaranteed birdie. It is, after all, only 445 yards. While that is so, the landing area is restricted, and missing it with a drive means trouble. Woods line both sides, but landing between them means a better-than-average chance to go for the green, guarded in front with a sand trap.

No. 15 is memorable for the housing. Halfway down the hill, just left of the fairway on this 173-yard par 3, sits a cabin that is more than a century old. While we are generally death on SVPs (stupid vacation pictures), for this, as with the chimney next to the green, we made an exception.

ACCOMMODATIONS

Cacapon Resort State Park   (304) 258-1022
818 Cacapon Lodge Dr., Berkeley Springs, WV
ROOMS: 48; **SUITES:** 30
ROOM RATES: $65 + $6 each additional person   **PAYMENT:** checks, MC, VS, AX, DIS, DC
SPECIAL RATES: seniors: 10% discount
RESTAURANTS: various restaurants available (entrees range from $9–$18)
RESORT AMENITIES: cable TV/movies, smoking rooms, non-smoking rooms, conference facilities
CONFERENCE/BUSINESS MEETING FACILITIES: can accommodate meetings and seminars

GOLF

GOLF PACKAGE RATES: $173–$248 for 3 days and unlimited rounds
PACKAGE INCLUDES: greens fees only; Sun–Thu packages available

COURSE:

Cacapon Mountain Golf Course   (304) 258-1022
U.S Rte. 522, Berkely Springs, WV

OTHER ATTRACTIONS NEARBY

Galleries, craft shops, community theater, professional performances, art exhibitions at the Ice House, summer concerts in the park

DIRECTIONS

I-80 east; east on I-76 to Breezewood; east on I-70 to Hancock, MD/Berkeley Springs; south on SR-522 to WV; 10 miles south of Berkeley Springs.

MORGANTOWN, WV
LAKEVIEW RESORT

Ideal for a business retreat, and bring the family along

LOCATION: Northeast WV

DRIVE TIME: 3–4 hours

COST: $$$

....

STAY: The Lakeview Golf Resort & Spa, Morgantown, WV

PLAY: Lakeview Golf Course & Mountainview Golf Course, Morgantown, WV

NEARBY: West Virginia University

This is a resort for the family, for couples, for golf groups, and for business conferences. Here guests have two first-class golf courses and views that inspire awe. Welcome to Lakeview Golf Resort & Spa.

It sits peacefully in the foothills of the Allegheny Mountains, hard by Cheat Lake. The resort was built in 1954. Lakeview, one of its two courses, was also built then. The resort started with 30 rooms; it has grown to 187. Fifty condominiums have been added. Reservations are highly recommended, and we're not talking about a couple of weeks. We're talking a couple of months.

Lakeview's CMP—Complete Meeting Package—covers all costs associated with a meeting: food, lodging, continuous service breaks, et al. The meeting space here can accommodate up to 600 people. It includes 23 meeting rooms, a 12,500-square-foot convention center, and 23,000 square feet for small- and mid-sized groups. The place is only ten minutes from Morgantown, home of West Virginia University.

If you're wondering when we're going to get to the golf, relax. This place is so nice for business, we longed for the good ol' days, when we had real jobs and once or twice a year had to create conferences. Why, oh why, didn't we know about this place?

Rooms are spacious and well-equipped. Two pools, one indoors and one outdoors, and a 30,000-square-foot fitness and sports center are here. Is this what golf resorts have come to, we wondered? In the fitness building is a climbing wall, racquetball and basketball courts, whirlpools, indoor/outdoor tennis . . . it doesn't end. There is the Spa Roma, which offers hair services, massage, and all sorts of stuff done to your body. The restaurant service and food was very good, though we wondered if the view of Cheat Lake influenced us.

We thought later we should have asked to stay a week or so. The kids are welcome and can be deposited at Lakeview Kids Club. The club is designed to keep kids age 4 to 12 busy while parents enjoy themselves.

Speaking of kids, there is plenty to do elsewhere in the area: rock climbing (at Cooper's Rock State Park), whitewater rafting, boat and bike rentals, winery tours, museums, and some very pretty walking trails.

For all that this resort offers, it is the two main acts, Mountainview and Lakeview golf courses, that get curtain call after curtain call. Guess

GOLFERS PLAY 70,000 ROUNDS A YEAR ON THE TWO COURSES who played here before you? Patty Berg, Steve Elkington, Byron Nelson, Jack Nicklaus, Gary Player, Arnold Palmer, Curtis Strange, and Jan Stephenson.

Golf outings at the courses here can be scheduled a year in advance. Golfers play 70,000 rounds a year on the two courses, and keeping them in the shape we found them must be a challenge.

THE GOLF

In 1999, Lakeview was closed for the first time in 45 years. A restoration project was launched to boost the quality of the course. It was successful; *Golf Digest* awarded it four stars.

J. D. Gump, the golf sales manager, said it's "A traditional golf course. No trick shots needed. Just hit it straight off the tee, and be accurate from there on in." Easier said than done, of course. The blue tees go 6,670 yards; whites, 6,357; reds, 5,432. There is no water to contend with on the course.

The story here is large greens: big, undulating, true, and fast. For players more rash than thoughtful, they can kill. Gump said, "The entire golf course does not have one easy hole. There's not that one hole to get back a stroke or stop the bleeding."

Nos. 3 and 6, a pair of par 4s, are fraternal twins, the former measuring 376 yards, the latter an even 400. Both tees are close, and the tree-lined fairways slope from right to left. Flying the greens means tumbling down a ravine. The views of Cheat Lake are noteworthy.

No. 7, a 541-yard par 5, drops 180 feet from tee to green. *Golf Magazine* said it was like, "teeing off from atop an 18-story building." The home hole is a 602-yard par 5 that goes up. This par 5 has never been reached in two. (And with Tiger Woods's management company, IMG, charging $1.5 million for appearances, it's not likely the boy wonder will tee it up here.)

It's a dogleg left. From a level tee box, the landing area is open and flat. Then it's fun time. The second shot begins the uphill climb and gets steeper as it goes. The tree-lined fairway narrows at some points, and the green is cut into a small hill in front of the main lodge. It is trapped right and left.

Although the Mountain Course is first cousin to Lakeview, the similarities are few. When it was built in the 1980s, "target golf" was a favorite design style. While length rarely hurts here, loading the driver and firing away is not the way to play best. Between the narrow landing areas and canted fairways, keeping the ball away from trouble becomes important.

The course is five minutes from the lodge, and with its small, trailer-style clubhouse, we wondered about the quality. Now we don't know why. Every hole is a good hole, and each has a personality. The blues measure 6,447, the whites, 6,152, and the reds, 5,385. Conditioning was very impressive. Fast greens with hidden breaks made us three-putt more often than usual.

On many of the holes, the view is just spectacular. This is the course to take your camera and your zoom lens.

No. 9 is 505 yards from the blues, and the tee shot is uphill. The canted fairway goes right to left. The second shot has to find a smaller landing area, and it gets tighter the closer to the green. The green is cut into the side of a hill and tough to hold as it slopes back to front.

No. 13 is another tough one: a 391-yard par 4 with a landing area the size of your neighbor's swimming pool. No. 15 tees off over a ravine before turning to the right. If you're on in two here, you're a shotmaker.

The home hole is a 549-yard par 5, with a narrow, canted fairway. The 150 yard marker is at the crest of a hill, and everything between that spot and the green is steeply downhill.

Mountainview may never have the reputation Lakeside has, but it will have a favored spot in the memories of many, many players.

OTHER STATES : WEST VIRGINIA

ACCOMMODATIONS

The Lakeview Golf Resort & Spa   (800) 624-8300
One Lakeview Dr., Morgantown, WV

ROOMS: 187; **SUITES:** 50

ROOM RATES: $89–$325   **PAYMENT:** checks, MC, VS, AX, DIS

SPECIAL RATES: AAA, AARP

RESTAURANTS: Reflections (avg. entree $17), Sportsview (avg. entree $11), Leaderboard (avg. entree $11)

RESORT AMENITIES: indoor pool, outdoor pool, health club, sauna, hot tub, cable TV/movies, room service, smoking rooms, non-smoking rooms, babysitting service, conference facilities, full spa/salon

CONFERENCE/BUSINESS MEETING FACILITIES: 23 meeting and conference rooms, a 12,500-square-foot convention center, 23,000 square feet of function space, and conferencing space for up to 600

SPECIAL PROGRAMS FOR CHILDREN: Lakeview Kids Club offers daily activities for children of all ages including nature hikes, crafts, face painting, water games, swimming, and more

GOLF

GOLF PACKAGE RATES: $129–$169 for 1 day and 2 rounds

PACKAGE INCLUDES: food/beverages, cart rental; weekend packages available; Sun–Thu packages available

COURSES:

Lakeview Golf Course & Mountainview Golf Course   (800) 624-8300
One Lakeview Dr., Morgantown, WV

OTHER ATTRACTIONS NEARBY

Cooper's Rock State Park, Cheat Lake, West Virginia University, Rails to Trails, Fallingwater, white water rafting

DIRECTIONS

I-80 east; east on I-76; east on I-79 to exit 152 for Morgantown; left on US-19; right on County Hwy. 73; left on County Hwy. 12; left on County Hwy. 67; left on Mark's Dr.; right on Alexandria's Dr.

PARKERSBURG, WV
BLENNERHASSET
& WOODRIDGE
PLANTATION

A National Historic Landmark hotel
with a AAA Four-Diamond restaurant

LOCATION: Northwest WV

DRIVE TIME: 3–4 hours

COST: $$

....

STAY: Historic Blennerhassett Hotel, Parkersburg, WV

PLAY: Woodridge Plantation Golf Course, Mineral Wells, WV

NEARBY: Blennerhasset Island State Park

Thanks to lumber, oil, and natural gas, Parkersburg, West Virginia was booming in 1889. The Blennerhassett Hotel opened that year, built by William N. Chancellor. It continues to provide service today. Gary Wolf, a native to the area who does a lot of local community work and investing, manages the place. He's a former prizefighter and referees professional matches throughout the country.

The brass chandelier in the lobby is more than a century old, having been converted from natural gas to electricity. The grandfather clock—imported from England, is a great-great-grandfather, more than 150 years old. Even the door to the coat room has a history—a Pennsylvania Dutch original now 113 years old.

The hotel was fully restored in 1986; it has since been registered as a National Historic Landmark. The original building has fifty-odd guest rooms located around the central staircase. The kitchen was on the fifth floor.

The staircase is no longer there, and guest accommodations have grown to 104 rooms and three luxury suites. The kitchen has been returned to a more sensible location, next to Harman's, the highly-acclaimed restaurant on the first floor. For five consecutive years, Harman's has been honored with AAA's 4-diamond rating. And it's not the only restaurant; there is also the American Harvest Cafe.

In addition, conference/meeting space can serve up to 300 in the ballroom, 50 in a pair of meeting rooms, and 22 in the boardroom.

The Oil and Gas Museum is in Parkersburg, and so is the Blennerhassett Museum, which chronicles the lives and times of the movers and shakers for whom the hotel was named. A stern wheeler will take guests to Blennerhassett Island, on the Ohio River, where the family mansion remains. There are wagon rides, bikes for rent, hiking trails, and spots for picnics.

As long as we're in the neighborhood, no sense passing up a tour of the Fenton Art Glass Company. *USA Today* says the factory tour is one of the best, and while we don't know their criteria, we do know this: it's fascinating and well worth the time and effort.

There are also tours of haunted Parkersburg. The Banshee of Marrtown, the Mothman, the Weeping Woman who walks at midnight ... and Bean-Sidhe, the Scottish death fairy who forewarns the living of impending danger. And you thought *your* neighborhood was rough.

Remember when college athletes were jokingly accused of taking basket-weaving courses? Well, basket-weaving is taught by The Friends of Blennerhassett. This is true. Last fall, master basket-weaver Gary Anderson taught the course at the Blennerhassett Museum.

Between the ghostly tour, the Fenton tour, and the basket-weaving classes, a family could have a great time in Parkersburg even if the clubs were left at home. Not our family, of course, but lots of families. Parkersburg takes advantage of what it has—a great history and an enthusiastic group of supporters.

THE GOLF

The Blennerhassett has golf packages with a number of good courses. We played Woodridge Plantation Golf Club, which opened in 1992.

John Salyers designed this course on 140 acres, and he has Bermuda grass in the fairways, Pennlinks-bentgrass on the greens, and 72 sand bunkers.

It can play long: the black tees measure 6,830 yards, the blues go 6,467, the white are 6,086, and the reds are 5,031. He used mounding on many holes, which helps visually define the hole for the player as well as prevent balls from bouncing away from the fairway. The fairways roll and are often bordered with high grass. At times, the look is Scottish links. The greens are undulating, tiered, and beautifully conditioned. Tough to putt the first time out, but true. Ten holes have doglegs, many of them close to 90 degrees.

The designer comes to mind on the third tee, a 153-yard par 3 built into the side of a mountain. On the left are woods and high grass waving insolently at players. On the right ... well, the right falls off the mountain. The green is long and narrow.

At the sixth tee, a 358-yard downhill par 4, there appears to be a tree in the fairway. It's actually to the right of the fairway and an excellent target. Accuracy is rewarded here, because the fairway zooms left for the approach.

No. 14 is a delicate par 4 of 291 yards. Between the approach and the green is substantial water along the right side. That same water has a more important role in the next hole, another short par 4, this one 370 yards. The dogleg turns right and hugs the lake almost the entire distance.

The home hole is a 525-yard par 5, and for our money it's one of the best finishing holes anywhere. To reach the corner of the dogleg calls for a 225-yard drive. The second shot has to carry a creek with trees right and O.B. left, and it's no easy shot—180 yards of carry. Having successfully hit those two shots, it's cake.

We finished, looked back, and said, "There's not a boring minute on the entire course." We're not alone is our high praise: the West Virginia Junior and Senior State Championships are determined here, and *Golf Digest* was similarly impressed. It called Woodridge Plantation "a course with character, a fantastic place to play, with excellent greens."

We second the motion.

THERE'S NOT A BORING MINUTE ON THE ENTIRE COURSE.

ACCOMMODATIONS

Historic Blennerhassett Hotel   (304) 422-3131
320 Market St., Parkersburg, WV

ROOMS: 104; **SUITES:** 4

ROOM RATES: $69–$120   **PAYMENT:** checks, MC, VS, AX, DIS

RESTAURANTS: Historic Blennerhassett Hotel

RESORT AMENITIES: indoor pool, health club, sauna, hot tub, cable TV/movies, room service, pets welcome, smoking rooms, non-smoking rooms, conference facilities

CONFERENCE/BUSINESS MEETING FACILITIES: four conference and meeting rooms accommodating up to 300 guests.

GOLF

GOLF PACKAGE RATES: $169 for 2 nights for 3 days and 3 rounds

PACKAGE INCLUDES: greens fees only

COURSE:

Woodridge Plantation Golf Course   (304) 489-1800
301 Woodridge Dr., Mineral Wells, WV

OTHER ATTRACTIONS NEARBY

Blennerhasset Island State Park, Cultural Center of Fine Arts, Smoot Vaudeville Theater, Oil and Gas Museum, Ruble's Sternwheelers (riverboat trips), Lee Middleton Doll Factory, Fenton Art Glass (factory, museum & outlet)

DIRECTIONS

I-77 south to exit 176 for SR-50; west on SR-50 to Market St.; left on Market; on left at the corner of Market and 4th St.

WHEELING, WV
OGLEBAY RESORT

*More than just a weekend's
worth of stuff to do*

One hundred fifty miles of highway connect Cleveland to Oglebay Resort and conference Center in Wheeling, West Virginia. There is a more substantial connection than asphalt and state troopers: the property for the 1,650-acre resort was donated by Cleveland businessman Earl W.

LOCATION: Northwest WV
DRIVE TIME: 2–3 hours
COST: $$

STAY: Oglebay Resort & Conference Center, Wheeling, WV
PLAY: Spiedel Golf Club at Oglebay, North Wheeling, WV

Oglebay. When he died in 1926, his vacation property was willed to Wheeling, which owns it today and operates it via the Wheeling Park Commission.

Wilson Lodge opened in 1957. Expanded over the years, it now has 212 deluxe guest rooms. In addition, 48 spacious cottages, each with a fully equipped kitchen, are available. The cottages come in two-, four-, and six-bedroom models.

Wilson Lodge also has an indoor pool, a Jacuzzi, a Wolfe tanning bed, a fitness center, and in-room massage services. With all of that, it serves the business community as well, with more than 20,000 square feet in 15 meeting rooms.

Dining at the Lodge begins in the spacious and elegant Ihlenfield Dining Room. This multi-level restaurant served us great food, and they do it many different ways, including buffet, gourmet, and kids' meals. The view is as good as the food; the dining room overlooks Schenk Lake and surrounding hills and valleys.

A couple of other options worthy of mention: the Glassworks Grill has snacks and lighter items, and the Pool Cafe serves it up fast.

Crispin Center is one of the most popular venues at Oglebay. Built in the late 1930s of sandstone, the facility has 11 tennis courts and a huge outdoor swimming pool.

Lots of city slickers enjoy horseback riding here—lessons and guided tours are available. The stables also have day camps for kids seven to fifteen.

Since 1930, the Oglebay Institute has been offering programs in four fields: environmental education, visual arts, museums, and theater. The Institute has grown over the years, and now has a cinema with the largest screen in the area, a wonderful dance program, and educational programs for area schools. Families most welcome.

Schenk lake is only three acres, but it has lighted water shows with 150-foot plumes of water. Boat rentals, fishing, miniature golf, and playground are all there.

To see animals (other than the guys you're playing with), there is Oglebay Zoo, where 85 different species live behind bars on a 30-acre tract of gorgeous hills and valleys filled with hardwoods and wildflowers. The historic C. P. Huntington train ride chugs along for a mile and a half through a grassland exhibit, and there's the Discovery Lab, where kids (and you) learn more about animals.

THE GOLF

Golf at Oglebay features two great championship courses, one by Robert Trent Jones and the second by Arnold Palmer. There is also Crispin, the 50-year-old track that chugs up and down hills for 5,670 yards of very challenging target golf. There is also a pitch-and-putt course and a mountaintop driving range.

All golf facilities are near Wilson Lodge; the two championship courses share a clubhouse. Caddies are available form June to August, but call and make arrangements before you set off.

The Jones course used to be a regular stop for the LPGA Tour. The West Virginia Classic was played here from 1974 to 1985.

The Jones course, in addition to lots of other virtues, has the toughest three finishing holes we've seen since we caddied at Canterbury. Three par 4s: 398, 414, and 396 yards respectively. No. 16 is a slight dogleg right with the fairway sloping down right to left. Woods line the right side, and a large sand trap waits on the left side of the landing area. The green is built up, and big sand guards the left side.

On No. 17, the driving area slopes down left to right and has woods at the bottom. The green is cut into the base of a hill and is bunkered in front. The home hole is scary: this big dogleg calls for a drive carrying 225 yards. A deep ravine yawns on the left side of the fairway from the elbow to the green. It is insatiable. The green here is tough as well—long and narrow, in the shape of a boot print.

While the course is a challenge, it's also exhilarating. Dramatic side-hill shots, a premium on staying in the short grass, and the drama of the hills make for a memorable round. Greens are fast.

There are five sets of tees here, and on the scorecard are tee recommendations by handicap. For example, if your handicap is between 10 and 24, the white tees are for you.

At the Palmer course, the King himself came to play the dedication round on May 4, 2000. Palmer's design is markedly different from Jones's but equally delightful. The Palmer design, it appears, is more player-friendly, a members' course, if you will. Fairways are mounded, and high grasses run throughout. The sand traps here are deeper than most, a fact made more clear with every swing it takes to get out. Greens are well trapped and very fast; many feature hogbacks. For all the hills here, none of the holes play uphill.

From the No. 4 tee box, players get a view so spectacular it can slow play: 13 holes can be seen in this panorama.

Go on, hitch up your trousers.

OTHER STATES : WEST VIRGINIA

ACCOMMODATIONS

Oglebay Resort & Conference Center   (800) 752-9436
Rte. 88 North, Wheeling, WV

ROOMS: 212; **SUITES:** (cottages) 49

ROOM RATES: $120–$155   **PAYMENT:** checks, MC, VS, AX, DIS, DC

SPECIAL RATES: package rates available

RESTAURANTS: Dining Room at Wilson Lodge (avg. entree $17), Restaurant at Spiedel Golf Club (avg. entree $6), Glass Works Grill at Wilson Lodge (avg. entree $6)

RESORT AMENITIES: indoor pool, outdoor pool, health club, sauna, hot tub, cable TV/movies, pets welcome in cottages, smoking rooms, non-smoking rooms, babysitting service, conference facilities, specialty shops

CONFERENCE/BUSINESS MEETING FACILITIES: 15 meeting/conference rooms accommodate 1–500; banquet options to 500 people

SPECIAL PROGRAMS FOR CHILDREN: 30-acre zoo, model train exhibit, planetarium, train ride, discovery lab, stables and trail rides, paddle boats, miniature golf, swimming, environmental education center, discovery trails

GOLF

GOLF PACKAGE RATES: call to put together package for variable number of days and variable number of rounds

PACKAGE INCLUDES: details available on request

COURSE:

Spiedel Golf Club at Oglebay   (800) 752-9436
Route 88, North Wheeling, WV

OTHER ATTRACTIONS NEARBY

Wheeling Island Race Track & Gaming Center, WV Independence Hall, Kruger Street Train & Toy Museum

DIRECTIONS

I-77 south to Columbus; east on I-70 to exit 2A; north on SR-88.

NIAGARA FALLS, CANADA
NIAGARA FALLS

*Niagara Falls provides
a diversion and a backdrop*

LOCATION: Canada
DRIVE TIME: 3–4 hours
COST: $$$

STAY: Sheraton Fallsview, Niagara Falls, Canada
PLAY: Legends on the Niagara, Niagara Falls, Canada
NEARBY: Niagara Falls,

First we must admit that out of 50 getaways we actually went to only 49—because this one, The Legends of Niagara, wasn't even open for business yet when we did our research. But we'll be among the first from Northeast Ohio to jump in the car and head east now that it is.

Getting there is easy. If you can find Buffalo, you can find the Peace Bridge, and signs take you the rest of the way. Just to be on the safe side, disavow any knowledge of the song "Blame it on the Canadians."

This wonderful getaway has two things other getaways don't. First, Niagara Falls. How could you not enjoy a getaway with one of Mother Nature's greatest displays, rumbling and hissing right outside the hotel window? Second, the Niagara Parks Commission. Their history with golf courses is sterling.

The Sheraton Fallsview provides, it will not surprise you, the most exciting view from any hotel window. It is, at 32 stories, the tallest hotel to overlook the falls. You don't know what a rainbow is until you see a Niagara Falls rainbow. There are 402 guest rooms here, and it has been named a Four-Diamond hotel by the Automobile Association for each of the last 10 years.

Niagara-on-the-Lake and the Shaw Festival Theatre are close by, and shuttle service is provided to Casino Niagara.

The Niagara Park's Commission operates Whirlpool Golf Course and Oak Hall Golf Course; they, with Legends (which is two courses, Battlefield and Ussher's Creek) make up the Niagara Parks Golf Trail. The Legends is on the banks of the Niagara River.

Canadian PGA Master Professional Tony Evershed was at the IMG golf show this year. The new courses, he said, were designed by the two best Canadian designers: Doug Carrick, who did Battlefield, and Thomas McBroom, who did Ussher's Creek.

Battlefield is named for an American victory over the British in the Battle of Chippewa. Ussher's Creek is named for the snake-like waterway that makes its presence known throughout the course.

We're eager to get to the new clubhouse, which cost a mere ten mil to put up and features a 250-seat dining room as well as a gorgeous balcony overlooking the home hole. The structure will be built from Ontario stone and rough-hewn cedar. We're looking forward to meeting chef Barry Burton and Cathy Sherk LPGA, whose exploits as an amateur make good reading—in the record books!

ACCOMMODATIONS

Sheraton Fallsview   (800) 267-8439
6755 Fallsview Blvd., Niagara Falls, Canada

ROOMS: 402; **SUITES:** 47

ROOM RATES: $89–$1,200 **PAYMENT:** MC, VS, AX, DIS, DC

SPECIAL RATES: Seniors, AAA, website specials (www.fallsview.com)

RESTAURANTS: Fallsview Dining Room (avg. entree $17)

RESORT AMENITIES: indoor pool, fitness room, cable TV/movies, room service, smoking rooms, non-smoking rooms, conference facilities, airport shuttle

CONFERENCE/BUSINESS MEETING FACILITIES: 35,000 square feet of meeting rooms

GOLF

GOLF PACKAGE RATES: starting at $325 for 1 day and 1 round

PACKAGE INCLUDES: breakfast, cart rental; weekend packages available; Sun–Thu packages available

COURSE:

Legends on the Niagara   (905) 295-9595
9233 Niagara Pky., Niagara Falls, Canada

OTHER ATTRACTIONS NEARBY

Niagara Falls, Niagara Parks, Rainland, IMAX theater

DIRECTIONS

I-90 east to Peace Bridge; north QEW to McCloud Rd; east on McCloud; left on Stanley Ave.

INDEXES

ALPHABETICAL INDEX

I N D E X E S

IDEA INDEX

Cost: $

Berkeley Springs, WV, Cacapon Resort, 179
Bolivar, PA, Champion Lakes, 142
Edinboro, PA, Culbertson Hills & Riverside, 148
Gibsonia, PA, Sun & Cricket & Deer Run, 155
Marietta, OH, Marietta & Oxbow, 87
New Philadelphia, OH, Oak Shadows, 27
Warren, PA, Blueberry Hill & Jackson Valley, 169
West Middlesex, PA, Yankee Run, 172

Cost: $$

Ann Arbor, MI, Weber's Inn & Reddeman Farms, 111
Archbold, OH, Sauder Village, 42
Beaver Falls, PA, Black Hawk, 135
Blairsville, PA, Chestnut Ridge & Tom's Run, 138
Cambridge, OH, Salt Fork Resort, 80
Canton, OH, Legends & Tam O'Shanter, 19
Celina, OH, Fox's Den, 45
College Corner, OH, Hueston Woods Resort, 90
Columbus, OH, New Albany Links, 59
Friendship, OH, Shawnee Resort, 94
Hamilton, OH, Hamiltonian & Shaker Run, 97
Hidden Valley, PA, Hidden Valley Four Seasons Resort, 159
King's Island, OH, King's Island, 102
Logan, OH, Cedar Falls & Brass Ring, 83
Meadville, PA, Whispering Pines & Oakland Beach, 162
Mt. Sterling, OH, Deer Creek Resort, 69
Newbury, OH, Punderson Manor Resort, 31
Norwalk, OH, Eagle Creek, 52
Parkersburg, WV, Blennerhasset & Woodridge Plantation, 187
Perrysville, OH, Mohican & Chapel Hill, 77
Titusville, PA, Cross Creek Resort, 165
Wheeling, WV, Oglebay Resort, 191
Wilmington, OH, Majestic Springs, 105
Wooster, OH, Hawk's Nest, 39
Ypsilanti, MI, Eagle Crest Resort, 120
Zelienople, PA, Inn on Grandview & Olde Stonewall, 175

Cost: $$$

Battle Creek, MI, Gull Lake View, 116
Boardman, OH, Mill Creek & Reserve Run, 15
Champion, PA, Seven Springs Mountain Resort, 145
Chautauqua, NY, Chautauqua Institution, 123
Columbus, OH, The Lofts & Cook's Creek, 62

Concord, OH, Renaissance Quail Hollow Resort, 23
Dublin, OH, Dublin & Darby Creek, 66
Ellicottville, NY, Holiday Valley Resort, 127
Farmington, PA, Nemacolin Woodlands & Mystic Rock, 151
Findley Lake, NY, Peek 'n Peak Resort, 131
Huron, OH, Sawmill Creek Resort, 48
Morgantown, WV, Lakeview Resort, 183
Newark, OH, Cherry Valley & Links at Echo Spring, 73
Niagara Falls, CANADA, Niagara Falls, 195
Oregon, OH, Maumee Bay Resort, 55
Sherrodsville, OH, Atwood Lake Resort, 35

Amish Country nearby

Canton, OH, Legends & Tam O'Shanter, 19
Ellicottville, NY, Holiday Valley Resort, 127
New Philadelphia, OH, Oak Shadows, 27
Perrysville, OH, Mohican & Chapel Hill, 77
Sherrodsville, OH, Atwood Lake Resort, 35
West Middlesex, PA, Yankee Run, 172
Wooster, OH, Hawk's Nest, 39
Zelienople, PA, Inn on Grandview & Olde Stonewall, 175

Amusement Park nearby

Battle Creek, MI, Gull Lake View, 116
Blairsville, PA, Chestnut Ridge & Tom's Run, 138
Bolivar, PA, Champion Lakes, 142
Champion, PA, Seven Springs Mountain Resort, 145
College Corner, OH, Hueston Woods Resort, 90
Hidden Valley, PA, Hidden Valley Four Seasons Resort, 159
Huron, OH, Sawmill Creek Resort, 48
King's Island, OH, King's Island, 102
Newbury, OH, Punderson Manor Resort, 31
Norwalk, OH, Eagle Creek, 52
Oregon, OH, Maumee Bay Resort, 55

Art/Galleries nearby

Archbold, OH, Sauder Village, 42
Berkeley Springs, WV, Cacapon Resort, 179
Boardman, OH, Mill Creek & Reserve Run, 15
Chautauqua, NY, Chautauqua Institution, 123
Columbus, OH, The Lofts & Cook's Creek, 62
Columbus, OH, New Albany Links, 59
Dublin, OH, Dublin & Darby Creek, 66
Edinboro, PA, Culbertson Hills & Riverside, 148

INDEXES

INDEXES

Pool, indoor

Pool, outdoor

Raceway nearby

Shopping nearby

INDEXES